CHILD O' WAR

CHILD O' WAR

The true story of a boy sailor
in Nelson's navy

RECREATED BY LEON GARFIELD

IN CONSULTATION WITH DAVID PROCTOR

Decorations by Antony Maitland

COLLINS
ST JAMES'S PLACE LONDON

TO TOM and PAT
and the ROYAL NAVY

ISBN 0 00 192165 7
© Leon Garfield and David Proctor 1972
First published 1972
Printed in Great Britain
Collins Clear-Type Press
London and Glasgow

Introduction

There's a fascination about old books; not just the withered brown leather and the thin, wrinkled pages that whisper to the touch – time does that to all of us – but the spirit of a book which survives unchanged while ours alters to suit our skin.

Take, for instance, this Memoir of Sir J. T. Lee in its frayed binding and its pressed, yellowing pages . . . Once it was spanking new, handsomely printed for the Author; maybe ten copies delivered to The Elms, Hampshire, to be inscribed and given into the hands of family and friends. Perhaps they read it (to see if they were mentioned), perhaps they didn't; for what was there about it to interest them? They knew Sir T. Lee – as he always called himself – and they knew the time he lived in, which was their own. So they shrugged and put the book away and drifted off into the future until at last they climbed into their deathbeds, kissed their children, bequeathed their property (together with the Memoir) and pulled the sheet up over their heads.

Inquisitive new hands took the book from the shelves . . . then put it back. Time had done nothing but render its grammar comical; it was old fashioned and not yet antique. So another generation left it where it was, and another and another, until at last time achieved the marvel of making the Memoir of Sir John Theophilus Lee interesting; not by changing the book but by changing the reader so that the age in which Sir T. Lee lived and wrote became almost legendary in its greatness and glory.

For this man lived right across a whirlwind of time. France exploded in revolution and threatened the world with bloody liberty. Napoleon Bonaparte blazed and died; Nelson and Wellington wrote their names across the age. It was the time of Beethoven, the great Goethe, Pushkin, Victor Hugo and the merciless Jane Austen. In Spain, Goya held up such a painted mirror to nature that nature was appalled; it was an age of giants . . . But it was also the age of Sir John Theophilus Lee, who was not a giant.

Nonetheless he crawled and toddled and trotted across his

time quite untroubled by the hugeness of it all. In a way he did what armies, policies, treaties and deep philosophies signally failed to do; he cut it all down to size and made it a backcloth for a portrait of himself.

He joined the Navy when he was five – much in the way a child might go to kindergarten. He went to sea at seven, was caught up in gigantic naval battles, sailed with privateers, met Lord Nelson and that great man's heart's mistress, Emma Hamilton, all before he was eleven. What a life – what a life! The heroes of a dozen romances had not a half of Sir T. Lee's opportunities! But Sir T. Lee was not the hero of other men's romances; he was the hero of his own. Not being of a dashing disposition, wisely he did not seek to dash; instead he rather minced, even crawled around the fringes of events . . . much as you and I do now.

But what else should a little man do in a great time? Should he admit himself to be a pigmy and tell his world how insignificant he really was? God forbid! A man must have his pride! So Sir T. Lee took his self-respect in both hands, summoned his family about him and bequeathed himself to history in a sarcophagus of handsome brown leather.

So now at last blow off the dust, open it up – and behold the Memoir of Sir John Theophilus Lee rise up from its grave.

Yet somehow it is not so much what he has written that lives again, but the circumstances of the actual writing. He gives no vital picture of his turbulent times, but rather a picture of his contented self, when, in 1836 he resolved to set down the strategy of his own particular triumph. Though he never describes the room in The Elms, nor his spellbound family, hanging on his every word, somehow that scene emerges more clearly than anything else.

The symbols ▶ ◀ *are used throughout this book to mark quotations from Sir J. T. Lee's original Memoir.*

CHAPTER ONE

1787 – 1795

In which Our Hero is born, treads on a bee, and the people of France roar into a Revolution that scorches the Old World and warms the heart of the more distant New. Danton, Marat and Robespierre rise and fall; tumbrils rattle, the guillotine flashes and heads are chopped off: commoners', princes' and even the King's. In the name of Liberty and Equality, France declares war on the Royal tyrants of Austria, England and Spain. England alone rides the storm; but her life-lines of trade are imperilled, and she can only survive by the might of the Royal Navy – in which our Hero now serves.

BORN of a sainted mother and a half-pay lieutenant in the Royal Navy at Modbury in Devon in 1787, Sir John Theophilus Lee has done uncommonly well for himself. He gazes round the spacious room at his family and rubs his hands together. But only in the privacy of his heart. Two of his daughters are taking his likeness and he has agreed not to move.

Eight children are present – five young women and three young men. There had been four more; but they took a fever and fell by the wayside and are so not able to be on hand. Somewhere in the room is the lady of the house; but Sir T. Lee cannot recall offhand in which shadow she is sitting . . .

The room is got up in the best of taste – a real forest of mahogany, beaked and clawed with glinting brass. The only indifferent objects in it are a number of nautical drawings hung round the walls; but even these are elegantly framed. They are the work of Sir T. Lee himself and, in an odd way, they reflect him; *he* is well-dressed too.

His small, sharp eyes, which resemble pistol muzzles, rake the walls and seem to fire little salutes at "The Battle of the Nile", "Martello Tower", and "H.M.S. *Swiftsure*" which looks like something between a paper hat and a Plymouth washerwoman.

Henrietta and Sophia Lee, who have inherited their father's graceful talent, bite their lips and rub out a portion of what they've drawn. Painfully divided between honesty and respect, they've done what they can for their model, but they've run aground over his right hand. It dangles over his left like five pork sausages. Abruptly their father's pistol muzzle eyes fix on them, and it's as much as the young women can do to stop themselves putting up their hands. Then there's a faint rustling and the pistol muzzles shift and take affectionate aim at Charlotte Augusta. All gauzy in the winter sunshine, she is waiting, quill in hand. Papa is dictating the story of his life.

Already she's written down the Dedication and the

interesting fact that it is all at "the earnest request of a lady and gentleman whose opinions have had great weight".

At this point there was some private conjecture as to who it was who could have had so dastardly an idea. Plainly, someone who wasn't coming back to sit through it all again.

But now the quill flutters on as Charlotte Augusta catches the words on the wing and neatly sets them down. It was 1789 and Papa was two.

Here, the assembled family dutifully try to see the enchanting little boy somewhere in the distinguished gentleman before them. They frown deeply, for here is the mystery of growth and time in which the grown man becomes the living sepulchre of the child.

The chief event of that year seems to have been the wilful murder of a humble bee by treading on it. But it was not the squelch he remembers so much as the remorse to which he was brought by his sainted mother. He wept for that humble bee; and even now, forty-six years later, as he remembers the little corpse by the wicket gate of the kitchen garden, slain by his own hand – or, rather, foot – a lump comes into his throat . . .

At about the same time, perhaps even on the self-same day, there was another sudden death. In Paris, the Governor of the Royal prison – the Bastille – had his head chopped off by an angry mob, and History, with bloody boots, had begun to tramp about the middle of the world. Suddenly, great men everywhere woke up and saw the opportunity of writing their names, with enormous letters, in other people's blood. With dauntless idealism and courage they hurled human beings at each other, and were generous enough never to count the cost. For the sake of simplicity, they lumped together the tens of thousands of husbands, fathers and lovers under the name of the country in which they lived and toiled and went home of a night-time to their children and wives. It seemed to lend a certain dignity to the proceedings and suggested – to the not over wise – that the very crops would benefit from the occasional shower of crimson rain . . .

By 1793 the great men had done so well that it was easier to say that half the world was at war than to begin to explain why multitudes of perfect strangers were blowing each other's brains out – and feeling proud to have done it. No one remembers them any-way; there was only enough blood in their veins to write out the most important names . . .

It was in 1793 that England, who was blessed with as many great men as the next country, plunged into the conflict, drawing her innocently cheering millions after her. Half-pay Lieutenant Lee was appointed to be first lieutenant aboard the *Royal Sovereign*. He and his family moved to Devonport and little John Theophilus joined the Royal Navy at the surprising age of five and a half. Even proud History sometimes dozes and lets the oddest things creep under its dripping gown . . .

▶ From this early period, ◀ says Sir T. Lee, referring to the supernaturally early age of his naval enrolment and not the antiquity of the event, ▶ little John Lee did not cost his parents a single shilling for his board, clothing or education – his daily allowance of pro-visions and a small, annual pay being more than adequate to his then trifling expenses. ◀

Here, while Charlotte Augusta gets it all down, he looks particularly hard at his sons, Melville and Alfred, whose expenses are not trifling. Having made his point, he goes on: ▶Weekly the little boy went by himself from the Dockyard on board the flagship of Sir R. King, bart. to be mustered; and all the officers knowing his father and family, he was uniformly invited to stay and dine in the ward-room, then considered no trifling indulgence, returning to the shore in the evening, blow high or blow low, greatly delighted with his day's *active* duty. ◀

Dreamily, the family contemplates the notion of the little boy, under cocked hat and tassels, the darling of the dockyard. Henrietta, the most imaginative, almost sees him and longs to pinch his rosy cheek and slap his chubby bottom, when, with a start of alarm, she recalls it is her Papa, and the impudent little darling scampers back into his stately selpulchre.

Unaware of this frivolous impulse in his eldest daughter, Sir T. Lee sails into 1795 when, at the advanced age of seven, he embarked at Plymouth on board the frigate *Eurydice*, ▶commanded by the late Sir John Talbot, K.C.B. to join his father, then first lieutenant of H.M.S. *Barfleur* at Spithead, about to proceed to the Mediterranean with the flag of Admiral the Hon. W. Waldegrave, since Lord Radstock, as second in command of the Mediterranean fleet, under the orders of Sir John Jervis, afterwards the immortal Earl St Vincent. ◀

As this necklace of gorgeous names drips from his smiling lips, an almost religious light shines in the muzzles of his eyes. He is very fond of lords; and, though second to none in his respect for Church and

Faith, there's little doubt that Sir T. Lee would have been happier if Our Lord had been a member of some more *definite* peerage.

▶ On the *Eurydice* passing the *Barfleur*, ◀ he continues with an air of soft and awed expectancy, ▶ to take up her anchorage at Spithead, little John was held up in the arms of the then Capt. Talbot, for the purpose of showing him to his father, who was observed to be anxiously looking out with a telescope, with a view to ascertaining if he were on board. The delight of young Lee at the new scene that now presented itself to his ardent imagination, no words can describe. ◀

Here, Sir T. Lee ventures a brief smile at the neatness with which he's managed to satisfy modesty and pride at one stroke. He always refers to himself as if he were another person, and an utterly enchanting one. ▶ No words can describe . . . ◀ he repeats, and toys with the vague memory of the floating cities, gleaming with paint and spired with cloud-piercing masts before regretfully abandoning it as a flight of fancy. Instead, he goes on with sterner stuff and so catches Charlotte Augusta unawares. Expecting a longer pause, she had neglected to ink her quill and so misses entirely several sentences in which little Lee boarded the *Barfleur*, got another cocked hat and little dirk, bade farewell to his dearest and best of mothers with almost as many tears as had been shed for the humble bee, and finally set sail with a fleet of six hundred merchantmen to play his part in the pageant of History. Nonetheless, she scratches away industriously and only she and her nearest sister see that their father's words are reduced to invisible ghosts. By the time she catches up with him, he and History have parted company. It is night-

time on the *Barfleur* and the infant sailor is somehow
in the ward-room, recovering from seasickness . . .

▶ lights being now brought in, some officers amused
themselves by playing billiards, on the rudder head,
while others sat down to a rubber of whist, all enjoying
themselves one way or another, till bed-time – the soft
tones of a flute, played by one of the officers, soothed
all into harmony and made him quite forget his malady
in the joyous feelings to which it gave rise.

After the novelty was worn off, he went to a sailor's
bed for the first time on board a ship of war, and
frequently were his slumbers broken by the noise of
the creaking of the beams, bulk-heads, gun-carriages,
and the noise of men continually moving about with
lanthorns employed on their multifarious occupations.
At early dawn the young sailor arose, and with difficulty, from the continual rolling of the ship, got on his
stockings and trowsers; but his jacket and shoes
having slipt out of his cot-clews during the night, to
search for them in his qualmish state was hopeless. He
therefore endeavoured to scramble on deck without
them, to try the effects of the refreshing morning air –
when a sudden pitch of the ship on his ascending the
ladder, brought on a violent return of the sickness,
from which he continued to suffer most severely for
three successive days. At this moment all his energetic
feelings, all his contemplated delights, all the anticipated honor of one day perhaps commanding himself
so fine a ship as that he then belonged to – vanished;
and he once more turned his mind to his dear and now
far distant parent, and sincerely longed to be again
leaning on her knee, and listening with delight to those
excellent admonitions her able and well regulated mind

felt such pleasure in bestowing, for the future guidance of her children. ◀

He stops. A faint but unmistakable sigh has discomposed him. It came from a profound shadow in the angle of the window and the wall. Lady Lee looks apologetic for having breathed so loudly. Sir T. Lee frowns. It is not the first time his wife has sighed when he's spoken of his sainted mother. He shakes his head as if to dispel an unjust thought – and decides that Lady Lee was sighing over his seasickness. He gives a gentle laugh as if to say that it was a long time ago . . . and like all calamities, passed to better things.

▶ At the end of three days the sickness gradually subsided, ◀ he says reassuringly, ▶ and the first occurrence that arrested the young sailor's attention as the squadron proceeded propitiously down channel, was the speaking with an American ship, the captain and seamen of whom he was quite astonished to find were white men, as he only knew the Americans by the black native usually employed to represent that country in books of geography; and would hardly credit but that all Americans were black. ◀

Charlotte Augusta's quill flutters frantically as Papa remembers more and more, some of which is even interesting. He remembers the regiments aboard the West India Convoy, and the music of their bands playing on distant decks on the calm, moonlit nights; he remembers the little sloops, plunging and dancing round the stately flagship; he remembers the arrival at Gibraltar when Spanish gunboats came out to attack, but did no such thing; and he remembers the little sailor he was, being already able to scramble as high as the maintop . . .

Involuntarily, Henrietta looks up as if expecting to see the tiny figure outlined against the marvellous Mediterranean sky, waving his hat wildly till he all but falls from the mast-head. But all she sees are some fine cracks in the ceiling; and Sophia nudges her back to the unsightly mess they have made of Papa's right hand. Something would *have* to be done . . .

CHAPTER TWO
1796 – 1797

In which the Revolution in France sinks from idealism to
politics and from enthusiasm to the shrewd calculation that
it is better for a hungry army to pillage foreign lands than
its own. Napoleon rises – and Italy falls. Spain declares war
on harassed England, and the Navy is stretched to its
uttermost in blockading the ports of France and meeting
the menace of Spain.

A SEA battle is in the offing – a mighty confrontation
of billowing ships of war. Sophia Lee despairingly
sketches what she hopes is a belaying pin in Papa's
horrible right hand. Henrietta giggles with helpless
impropriety. Sir T. Lee regards them sharply and the
young women go as red as ensigns. He has half a
mind to step across the room and overlook their work;
but thinks it might be taken for vanity . . . and he is

not a vain man. So he turns away and looks, with wistful satisfaction, at another of his lively representations on the wall. It is a battle scene; in fact, it is the very battle that he and his patient family are now approaching. His chest swells and his little eyes – now more like nine-pounders than pistols – seem to poke out from under their bushy ports in expectation of the blaze and bangs to come.

1797. History had assumed a frightful aspect. Another great man had arisen and had set about writing his name in letters that dwarfed the world: Napoleon Bonaparte.

To the discerning eye, the white cliffs of Dover went a shade whiter yet as England, proud little England, stood alone against the monster and faced a hostile world in arms. It was her darkest hour . . .

Not that the island itself had shifted in any way; nor had the sun failed more than usual to shine and bless the crops which continued, somewhat insensitively, to grow as if nothing was amiss.

Nor was this grand, historic darkness particularly offensive to the simple multitude who, as they always had, put up with their parents, kissed their children, and made love to their wives without a single thought for anything but each other.

It was the keen-eyed great ones who spotted it first, and patriotically passed it on; while they shivered in shoes that tomorrow somebody else might be filling.

Save England! went out the heartfelt cry, as if the very cliffs were crumbling and the whole sweet land was sinking into the sea.

Save England! The cry rang out across the middle of the world and echoed in the well-appointed cabins

of the better class ships of war where Admirals awoke
from the appalling boredom of a fourteen-month
blockade of Toulon and saw the chance of adding
their names as bright footnotes to the particular page
History was on. Save England! and what better way
to do it than by enriching her annals with a few well-
born heroes!

Somewhere among the handsome, many-petalled
flowers that bloomed in the sea off Toulon harbour –
indeed, on the handsomest of all – was "our little
sailor", "our young Mid.", in a word, John Theophilus Lee, now a seasoned nine and a half and popping
his chest buttons with the best of them to answer his
country's call.

The long months that had passed since first he'd
been to sea had indeed seasoned him, even as the stout
oak of the splendid ships themselves had been matured
by weather and use. Already the child gave promise
of the man as the seeds had been planted, one by
one . . .

He'd dined with the Governor of Gibraltar; he'd
met that bold Captain Macnamara who was to fight a
duel with the brother of the Marchioness of Towns-
hend, no less; he'd got on, like a house on fire, with
the Ambassador to Florence; he'd attached himself,
clairvoyantly, to a plain Mr Brenton who had since
become Rear-Admiral Sir Jahleel Brenton, Bart.,
K.C.B.; and he'd visited a famous gallery belonging
to a Tuscan nobleman (whose name he'd unaccountably
forgotten) in which, among a crowd of unmentioned
masterpieces, he distinctly saw a bust of the Hon. Mrs
Damer. The little sailor was ready . . .

It was on the morning of St Valentine's Day 1797,

and a thick fog rolled over the sea off Cape St Vincent
so that each ship seemed to sail alone in a white and
secret world. From time to time the mist shifted enough
to show some weird part of the nearest ship, so that the
crowned golden lion brooding under the *Egmont*'s
bowsprit came and went like some formidable spirit of
the deep; likewise other figureheads made brief and
threatening appearances as if ancient gods of war were
abroad.

At ten o'clock the fog lifted, and the English fleet,
moving in two compact lines, saw the immense fleet of
Spain with which it had been invisibly sailing.

Seven and twenty ships of the line opposed fifteen.
But the fifteen had the advantage of expecting the
engagement, and of being commanded by an admiral
of striking ability. With extraordinary rapidity, they
turned and cut the Spanish line in two, leaving – a
mile to the windward – the mighty *Britannia* whose
hundred guns blazed out to prevent the Spaniards re-
uniting. Then the British fleet turned again and sailed
along the amazed Spanish line, cheering and firing
huge broadsides, so that it seemed, to the frantic
Spaniards, that they'd missed their course and were
sailing down a roaring hedgerow in Hell, full of scarlet
flowers that puffed iron seeds the size of cannonballs.

Before the broken Spaniards could escape to the
safety of Cadiz, they had lost four great ships, two of
which fell to a boarding party, led in person in the
heat and fury of the battle by a one-eyed commodore
called Nelson . . .

The victory was overwhelming. The call to save
England had been most nobly answered. The white
cliffs stopped crumbling and the island stopped sinking

. . . and great men once more put their shoes outside their doors to be cleaned without fear of someone else stepping into them. Gratefully, and in the name of the country (for it would have been somewhat costly to do it in their own) they rewarded all they decently could. Sir John Jervis was made Earl St Vincent, and a shoal of Admirals and Rear-Admirals were knighted and baronetted with almost delirious relief.

And what of little John Theophilus in the infernal uproar, when the air was full of howling iron and shrieks and roars and cheers? Anxious little Lee . . .

▶ In the middle of the action having visited his father, and finding him well and untouched, he now proceeded to Mr Brenton (afterwards Sir J. Brenton, etc.) who blackened with smoke and choaked with dust, entreated a glass of wine and water, which his attached young friend flew down the hatch-way from the main-deck to obtain; and thinking his worthy father would also feel a little of the same beverage acceptable, carefully brought them up a tumbler-full, which each declared to be the most refreshing and agreeable they had ever taken.

This trifling event so struck Mr Brenton, that he related the particulars to his good father, the late Admiral Brenton, who presented our little sailor with a handsome dirk and belt, in testimony of his conduct to his son in this memorable battle. This little dirk is still preserved, and will always be valued from the manner in which it was given. ◀

Here Sir T. Lee looks extraordinarily pleased with the part he played in the engagement (and for whom he played it), before he goes on to tell of an alarming incident aboard the *Barfleur* which might well have deprived the assembled family of their father before he'd become so. After the action, the guns had been housed and double-shotted and a seaman had fallen asleep over one of them. Then someone had pulled the line of the lock and the gun had gone off, blowing a hole in the side of the ship and setting the timbers on fire. The panic had been tremendous; but mercifully the wind had not been strong enough to fan the fire, and carpenters repaired the damage. ▶ But the wretch who pulled the trigger was never detected, ◀ concluded Sir T. Lee sternly, and peers about the room as if that ancient miscreant has somehow concealed himself there.

▶ After this action our young Mid. first saw an operation performed, and most anxiously he watched its progress, being the amputation of the leg of a poor Hessian, who joined the ship off Toulon, with several others of his countrymen, just escaped from a French prison. The incision of the knife, sawing of the bone, taking up the blood-vessels, and dressing of the stump were all effected, when a deadly sickness came over the young sailor . . .

Our narrator cannot quit the subject of this momentous battle, the first he ever had the honor to witness, and in which he was found on enquiry to be by far the youngest of Britain's sons engaged on this memorable day, without adding a few reflections . . . ◀

He does indeed add his reflections, but as these are all political and so have nothing to do with human beings, his family's thoughts drift and are inclined to boggle at the circumstance of the enquiry that uncovered the afore-mentioned interesting fact. Who asked? When – and how? Was it possible that signals were run up, from ship to ship? "Got anybody less than nine and a half aboard?" Then, when all the fleet had answered, "No", up went the signal from the *Barfleur*: "We have!"

Truly Sir T. Lee had written his name on a page in history — if not in blood, at least in crayon.

CHAPTER THREE
1797

In which the Kingdom of the Two Sicilies and Portugal still
link their fragile arms with England against the might of
Napoleon. The Navy victuals at Lisbon and Our Hero goes
a-privateering . . .

EUPHEMIA LEE, a younger daughter, creaks in her
chair as her eyes slide sideways to a tray of cakes and
wine that a servant has left discreetly on a table by
the window. She is a portly girl whose crimson silk
gowns, cruel Henrietta once remarked, were more
work for a sailmaker than for a dressmaker.

Her face, glazed with hunger, has all the bland
longing of a ship's figurehead. Irritably Sir T. Lee
divines that her mind is more on the cakes than with
her papa — her papa who has just managed to get on
board the captured *Salvador del Mundo*.

▶And there he was shown the *crimson silk* chair◀ he says pointedly ▶in which the Spanish admiral died; — the shattered state of this immense ship, and the mattings and congealed incrustations of hair, blood and brains, upon the sides, decks, and beams attested the havoc made among her crew . . .◀

Euphemia's complexion changes and her dreadful attention wavers from the cream-encrusted cakes as if she had had a sudden nightmarish vision of herself exploding with similar gruesome results. She resolves forthwith never to eat another cake . . .

Satisfied with his victory, Sir T. Lee returns to the fleet in good time to sail to Lisbon and anchor in the wide Tagus. It was there that grandpapa Lee fell overboard and had to be fished out by his men with a boathook. It was there that a pair of Portuguese pilots were bribed to run the *Windsor Castle* and the *St George* on to a shoal — for which act of treachery the Regent of Portugal sentenced them to be sawn between two boards; but the English Admiral obtained a mitigation of the punishment to transportation to the coast of Africa for life.

▶The Regent gave small but well-executed medals to the officers employed in the saving these two fine ships of war, with his bust in gold thereon, one of which was awarded to our young sailor.◀

Here Sir T. Lee permits himself a quiet smile of pride, though what part he played in the heroic salvage is not at all clear. The unworthy suspicion floats into Henrietta's mind that Papa got his medal either by a happy mistake or by dint of tugging at coat tails. Fiercely she tries to suppress it and concentrates her attention on Sophia's pencil which is now attempting to turn the ambiguous belaying pin into a flag.

While at Lisbon, the happiest of events befell the future Sir T. Lee.

▶One morning . . . Lord Proby, the Captain of one of H.M. sloops, came on board in a great bustle and told Captain Lee that his wife and daughter were arrived in a packet off Belam . . . Not a little delighted was our young sailor to again behold so unexpectedly in a foreign land, his dear, his tender mother, and his much loved sister. The happy meeting over, all the events which had occurred since parting with the best of parents were related with boyish glee, and received with that eager delight which might be anticipated from strong natural attachment. ◀

Suddenly Sir T. Lee stares hard at his pale wife . . . then signs to Charlotte Augusta to ink her quill . . .

A dear friend, Sir Isaac Coffin, Bart. had advised him to take some cruises on an active frigate. Sir Isaac Coffin was a commissioner of the dockyard at Lisbon, and therefore certain to remain ashore while little Lee went sailing off into the blue. Was it possible he'd grown wearied of the bright ingratiating little face shining at him wherever he turned?

The *Aurora* was the lucky ship, and its fortunate commander was a Captain Henry Digby (afterwards Admiral Sir H. Digby, K.C.B., heir to his uncle, the Earl of Digby). So off they went to cruise the northern coast of Spain.

▶She was then completely disguised as a merchant-man, for being one of the old eight and twenty's, she could consequently be no match in sailing with the enemy's privateers, and must therefore depend upon her success in capturing them, to the perfectness of the disguise which she assumed, whereby they were allured to their certain destruction. The *Aurora* usually stood on and off the land under easy sail, having her main-top gallant-yard across and fore and mizen top gallant masts on the deck, with small poles run through the caps and large vanes thereon, while old carriage wheels and large bags of straw representing packages of goods were placed conspicuously over her quarters – the guns being concealed by a piece of canvass, secured to the side; whereon were painted various 'quakers' – a denomination given by sailors to wooden guns; the *bonnet rouge* was also most liberally placed upon the heads of the carved figures at her head and stern, representing the goddess Aurora; so that in this equipment she had all the appearance of an old ship of war, converted into a Brazilman. ◀

She had not long to wait. On the very second day as she plodded her crafty way through the grey of the morning, who should she meet but a fine French brig of 16 guns, cheerfully going a-hunting?

At once the Frenchman, neat, trim and quivering with expectation, pounced on the lumbering merchant-man; imperiously ordered her to heave to, prepared to send a boat on board . . . and awaited the trembling reply with the nearest a ship can come to tapping its foot with impatience.

Then came the *Aurora*'s reply. Up went the tarpaulins and the dull-witted merchantman bristled with wicked cannons.

Somewhat embarrassed, the privateer struck its colours . . . though doubtless the captain's face retained a good deal of the red.

That night the grinning *Aurora* sent her, with a new crew, to Lisbon to be sold.

A few days later, Captain Digby at the masthead, in round jacket and trousers, with his glass slung at his back, spied a Spanish convoy, creeping along the coast under the guardianship of but a single armed vessel. Promptly the roving *Aurora* hoisted the Spanish colours and looked innocently anywhere but at the convoy. The happy convoy beamed and went its ways. Came the night; and in a peaceful, quiet darkness the convoy lapped and jogged along. Then, of a sudden, a ship that had crept among them cloaked in a silent blackness like the night itself so that it must have seemed like the dream of a vessel, the insubstantial phantom in the watch's eye, burst into a blaze of light!

Fierce loud cheering filled the air, and dreadful cannons winked and glinted their unmistakable command. Stand and deliver! Captain Digby, that very dashing highwayman of the seas, had taken his second prize.

▸ The prisoners were soon exchanged; – ladies, children, servants, households goods, tradesmen's effects, everything that can be conceived, formed the cargoes of the convoy . . . The gallant Digby on this, as on all similar occasions, giving up a suitable vessel to the ladies and children, to convey them to their destination, and retaining one of the friars as a hostage for his companions, until ransomed by bills on Lisbon, when he was dismissed with a sum of money sufficient to carry him to his destination. The little convoy was now manned, and the *Aurora* proceeded with them . . . ◂

On the very next day there appeared a dapper brig of war. It spied the shabby old *Aurora* shambling along

with her prizes like some aged, down-at-heel chaperone
. . . At once this dapper brig twirled its fine French
moustaches and roguishly gave chase to the fat lady and
her choice possessions. Chase guns were fired and the
Aurora all but knelt in the sea for mercy from the
dashing Frenchman. Gaily he danced close, sidling for
the kill.

Alas for the gay Frenchman! Once more the *Aurora*
lifted up her tarpaulin skirts and displayed an armament
most unladylike.

Glumly the Frenchman struck his colours and came
aboard, leaving his dapper brig as yet another item in
the *Aurora*'s dowry. She turned out to be the sister ship
of the very first one captured, and their two captains
met, with fury and astonishment, on the *Aurora*'s deck.

By now the *Aurora* was uncomfortably full of Frenchmen and Spaniards and there was scarce anywhere to
put them; nonetheless, before reaching Lisbon, the
ever-willing Captain Digby spied a choice schooner
that suddenly hoisted the Portuguese colours and tried
to make off. Unimpressed, the *Aurora* pursued and
Captain Digby shrewdly observed that the schooner
was too well handled to be Portuguese. As usual, he
was right. It was a French schooner of war and it, too,
joined the *Aurora*'s private fleet.

The prizes were sold in a lump to the Jews at
Lisbon; ▶ And as soon as the gallant and active Captain
of the *Aurora* appeared there, he was surrounded by
competitors for the purchase of them, – the amount
being invariably paid down in cash, and divided before
another cruise commenced. This gave an eclat to the
Aurora which brought all the best seamen of the transports to enter on board her; and she had a ship's

company, for a vessel of her class, perhaps unrivalled in the service. Her crew became great dandies, having the gold Crusadoes made into buttons, and sewn so thick on their jackets, that many thousands of this coin were thus distributed in the ship. At the bottom of their trowsers they had also broad lace of fine quality; and, in fact, the *Aurora*'s men were known from all the other seamen of the fleet by these costly decorations, as well as by their large silver buckles, handsome silk handkerchiefs, and other clear indications of 'lots of prize money' . . . each man having received in the nine months our young midshipman belonged to *Aurora* about £600. ◀

Here a mistiness comes over Henrietta's eyes as she thinks of all that vanished glory, when sailors must have shone like birds of paradise, netted in the *Aurora*'s rigging. Bronze hard faces in a swirl of gorgeous silks; and the daintiest of laces kissing great naked feet. Such a juxtaposition of power and elegance sets Henrietta's heart a-fluttering, and she dreams of herself caught up in the gilded arms of such a lower deck man and hoisted into his languid hammock . . .

A rosy midshipman of scarce ten and a half comes to peer at her in her swinging nest – and sharply bids her lover begone. Lord have mercy! It's little Lee . . . Papa!

Abruptly Henrietta falls out of her dream hammock, for the *Aurora* is sailing again . . .

In her old disguise she shuffled off to her cruising ground where Captain Digby and his gaudy gang, or, rather, crew, began to repeat their past success when a dreadful thing happened.

Out of the early morning haze came two grim

shapes. Swiftly they grew in size and menace: a two-decker and a heavy frigate. And they flew the flag of France!

The *Aurora* was also flying the French flag, but it was unpleasantly plain that the approaching enemy was not deceived.

▶ The *Aurora* prepared for action; but as against such formidable odds, the struggle would necessarily be as short as ineffectual, our young sailor now deemed his naval career at an end, — with the certain horror of many a year's detention awaiting him in a French prison; he enquired of Captain Digby if he had not better equip himself with several shirts, waistcoats, and trowsers; as his chest and its contents by becoming a prize of his captors would leave him destitute of even a change. Capt. Digby advised him forthwith to do so, and off he ran, and returned on deck in a few minutes, with a face of broiling red, and streaming with perspiration in consequence of the heat of the weather, and the difficulty with which he moved about, so encumbered with clothes. ◀

By now, the *Aurora*'s crew were ready at their guns, to give a broadside before striking the colours. Lighted matches winked in the darkness of the ports, and multiplied themselves in the golden buttons of the gunners, and Captain Digby, now that gay privateering and cascades of prize money seemed a thing of the past, hastily bethought himself of the honour of old England. Down came the French flag and up went the English to float bravely from the mizen peak. The matches hovered, awaiting the order to fire, when —

The stranger hailed in English! The ships were as English as they themselves; each had been astutely

deceiving the other with their stolen French flags!
While greetings were being exchanged, ▶Our young
Mid. managed to disencumber himself of the shirts
and trowsers which had kept him in such a perspiration, — a story which Capt. Digby often afterwards
related, causing many a hearty laugh, at the expense of
the young Mid. ◀

At this point, young Melville Lee, who has somehow
managed to get halfway through his second glass of
claret, stares at his papa and sniggers helplessly. Sir
T. Lee frowns coldly. Merriment from the heir to the
Earl of Digby was one thing; from his family it is
quite another. Melville does his very best to straighten
his face; but it is plain that some internal heaving is
going on. Sir T. Lee thinks it a pity that Melville
has been denied the opportunity of being one of the
boys aboard the *Aurora*. It would have smartened him
up.

▶The boys on board the *Aurora* being placed ex-
clusively under the charge of our young Mid. were
mustered every morning by him, at seven bells, on the
quarter deck to ascertain that their faces and hands
were washed daily, and a clean shirt put on twice a
week; Capt. Digby observed on placing these boys
under the charge of young Lee, that of course he must
take care to show a good example of cleanliness and
neatness to them in his own person. At one of these
musters, the captain, whose vigilance could never be
evaded, observed one of the boys not so clean as he
ought to be, admonished the young Mid. to be more
strict in his examinations, and finding that the culprit
tried to palliate the neglect by telling an untruth,
forthwith ordered him to be tied up to the gun, and

flogged by the other boys. It was soon perceived, however, that they were favoring their colleague, on which the captain declared that the first who did not whip hard, should himself be tied up and punished; but the whole seeming to have combined, a second boy was soon elevated upon the next gun – then a third, fourth, fifth, and sixth, when the remainder finding the captain would not be played with, began to punish in earnest. This determination of the captain had a most salutary effect, as never after was there any want of cleanliness or irregularity of any kind, visible among the boys. ◀

Melville Lee spills his claret in attempt to conceal his grimy fingernails. There are a pair of ship's cannons in the porch of "The Elms", and he sees himself elevated on one of them and being soundly belaboured. From the tone in his papa's voice, the vision is shared by Sir T. Lee.

Then it passes and Sir T. Lee sighs. The ghost within him plucks at his heart with small fingers and reminds him that the time has come to leave the gay *Aurora* where gallant Captain Digby once told him he was the vessel's lucky star, and where, at dinner, the captain laughed and declared young Lee carved the pudding with peculiar grace; and where he found many another curiously bright memento that he'd all unknowingly laid up to be the present treasures of his deepest heart.

Such memories are like bottles of wine, casually acquired and left forgotten in a cellar for many years; then suddenly recalled to be brought to table where they spread the haunting fragrance of maturity . . .

The *Swiftsure* was his next ship and Captain Hallowell his new commander. His good friend, Sir Isaac Coffin had secured him a midshipman's rating – and pretty promptly, too. Sir Isaac seemed to have an interest in keeping the affectionate young sailor at sea. If little Lee's long absence had made Sir Isaac's heart grow fonder, it did not seem to be of his presence.

▶He was placed in the mess with the other midshipman under the care of a most worthy man, Mr Parr, the gunner of the *Swiftsure* who has since had three of his sons made captains in the navy. Here again . . . our midshipman had a truly attentive friend. Sir T. Lee even now feeling great pleasure when he can induce this worthy old seaman, who lives only a few miles from The Elms, to come and bring his respected wife, and spend the day with him and talk over past scenes. ◀

With mention of the Parrs, all the family, and especially Lady Lee, look pleased. They wish that gnarled and splendid couple would drive over more often in their trimly painted cart that seems to dance and sway up to the stately Elms like a lively sloop about a flagship. For when they come, and Mrs Parr gives sweets and sound advice to the younger Lees, and Mr Parr walks in the air with Midshipman Lee (that was), the world seems a better and more comfortable place . . .

▶The young sailor and his other new messmates soon became familiarly united, with one of whom, the brother of the present Lord Wharncliffe, (George Stuart Wortley), he afterwards formed a strong attachment. ◀

The family sighs. Papa is off again.

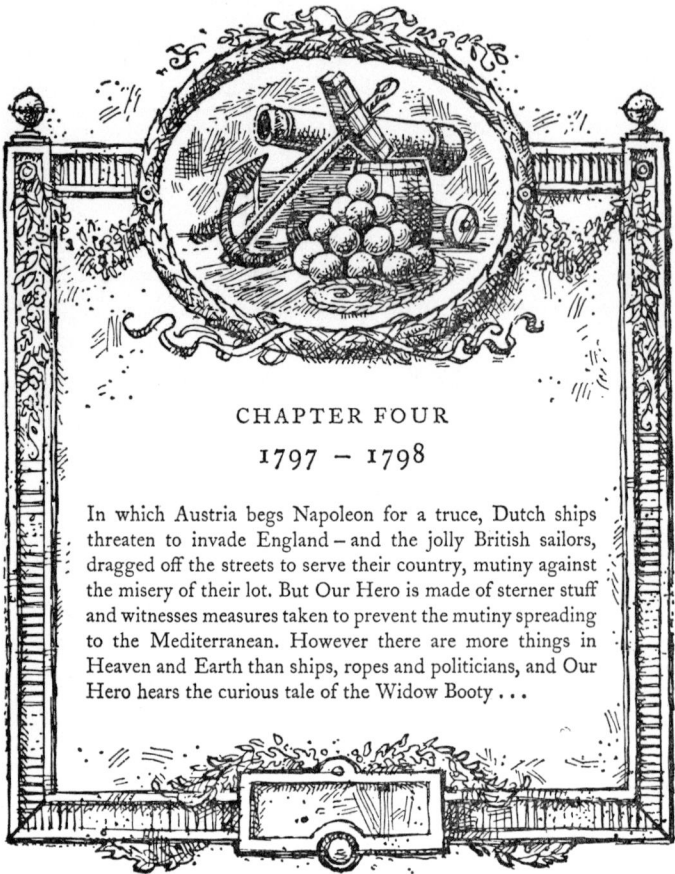

CHAPTER FOUR
1797 – 1798

In which Austria begs Napoleon for a truce, Dutch ships
threaten to invade England – and the jolly British sailors,
dragged off the streets to serve their country, mutiny against
the misery of their lot. But Our Hero is made of sterner stuff
and witnesses measures taken to prevent the mutiny spreading
to the Mediterranean. However there are more things in
Heaven and Earth than ships, ropes and politicians, and Our
Hero hears the curious tale of the Widow Booty . . .

MUTINY! At Spithead and the Nore the Fleet was in
mutiny. The seamen had not been paid and would not
go to sea unless they were.

England staggered under the treacherous blow.
After all, it was still her darkest hour . . . The mis-
creants who but yesterday had had the honour of
saving her, elected now to stab her in the back. For

money. Worse than Judas who was paid for betraying, they did it because they weren't. If only they'd had the sense of duty to wait until their country's danger had passed, when nobody but their wives would have needed them, then the Lords of the Admiralty could have hanged the lot of them with impunity. But alas! the sailors had been dastardly enough to press their claims for sufficient money to keep body and soul together at the one time when their living bodies were most desperately required. So an outraged Government — which would gladly have hanged the souls if it could have kept the bodies intact — was forced for once to listen to voices other than its own.

The mutiny grew apace, and even reached out abroad. Delegates from it sailed secretly on the *Princess Royal* and the fleet off Cadiz was in danger of the dread infection.

▶ To prevent the mutinous symptoms from attaining maturity among the squadron, all communication between the crews was as much as possible guarded against, and a strict eye kept upon the proceedings of the suspected delegates, as well as upon all such as were known to be intriguing and discontented, — the Admiral determined at the same time to terrify into submission, by making a severe example of the first individual, who showed a mutinous disposition. This opportunity was soon unfortunately afforded on board the *Swiftsure* in the case of a marine named Patrick McCrink, naturally a well-disposed man, but who seemed on this occasion to be inflamed by intoxication. In consequence of the difficulty of procuring water, strict orders had always been enforced, relative to economizing it; when McCrink, after having had two drinks at the scuttle-butt in a very short space, by permission of our young officer, then on watch, came a third time on the same errand, to the Lieut. of the watch, by whom he was refused. McCrink on this became insolent, and on the Lieut. threatening to put him in irons, broke out into very abusive language, for which he was ironed and gagged, on finding he still continued so violent. This affair having become very public through the fleet, it was deemed necessary to apply for a court-martial, which assembling the next day, and finding him guilty of mutiny, sentenced him to death. McCrink came on board his own ship after the trial, with an order from the Admiral for his execution, by being hanged at the yard arm the second morning after sentence.

It was a wet and foggy day, with the prospect of a gale from the westward, when the *Swiftsure* weighed and anchored amongst the main body of the fleet, whom the usual signal of an execution had prepared for what was to take place, — two boats from each ship, rowed by the most suspected hands, quickly assembled round the *Swiftsure*, when the rope to the yard arm being rove, young Lee was sent to the clerk's office, where McCrink was confined, under the care of two sentinels, to ask him if he was ready. The poor fellow's strength had been so prostrated by distress of mind that he could not stand without assistance, so that he was obliged to be led between two men to the larboard cathead, when the rope was fixed round his neck by the boatswain, a white cap placed on his head, and his legs and hands pinioned, — the captain desiring him to drop a white handkerchief when ready; but this he could not resolve to do, so that the fatal gun was obliged to be fired without it and McCrink was quickly run up to the yard arm, where he swung for an hour before being lowered down and consigned to the deep.

This prompt execution had a wonderful effect on the fleet; but the following act showed that Lord St Vincent dealt equal justice to both officer and man, – for not long after poor McCrink's execution, the boatswain of the *Emerald* frigate having uttered a few mutinous expressions was forthwith brought to a court-martial, sentenced to death, and twenty-four hours after hanged at the fore yard arm of his own ship, in his uniform coat; and two or three seamen of the *Prince George* sharing the same fate, all disposition to mutiny was thereby suppressed. ◀

A silence falls on the room. The winter sun casts the shadow of the window lattice on the wall beside Sir T. Lee, where it forms a cross; or a mast and yard.

▶ *A white cap was placed on his head . . .* ◀
Was this to hide his terror from his friends? Or was it to give him the privacy of a muslin bag in death while his good and lively body performed its monstrously public dance?

▶ *. . .* desiring him to drop a white handkerchief when ready; but this he could not resolve to do, so – ◀

Passionately the pale listeners saw his hands, formidably fierce in their grip on the white cloth. Nothing would have induced him to let go. So long as he holds it, he will live. He must have grasped it so tightly that very likely he cracked the bones of his fingers. How long did the executioners wait? How long did they stretch out his hopes before they shrugged their shoulders and stretched out his throbbing neck?

And what was in the mind of little Lee, scarce ten

years old, as he watched the morning sky being dis-
figured with the dark lifeless sack of Patrick McCrink?

Lady Lee stares at the calm contented face of her
husband and of a sudden understands that the vilest
crime a man can commit is against the sensibility of a
child; that crusading wars, the deeds of patriots and
heroes, and even the exhortations of saints, become as
foul as Hell when children suffer. The blasting of their
innocence and betrayal of their trust is the one crime
men can commit for which they are indeed answerable
to an angry God.

Then the sun goes behind a cloud and the cross
fades from the wall; but so powerful is its memory
that the pathetic end of Patrick McCrink, that well-
disposed man who went unwisely for a third glass of
water, lies heavily on all.

Melville Lee, sweating slightly, goes for his third
glass of claret, and stumbles over some irregularity of
the floor. Anxiously Lady Lee signs for him to take
something to eat as well, for it has been a long while
since breakfast; but Melville palely declines and returns to his station beside his brother Alfred and tries
to avoid his father's searching eye.

To his great relief and surprise, there is no particular
annoyance in it. In fact, the one he is looking at is
quite amiable. He cannot answer for the other as he
finds difficulty in taking in both of them at once.
Gently, Sir T. Lee shakes his head. He has remembered a certain occasion when Captain Hallowell sent
him ashore to purchase 250 gallons of Malaga wine
in Gibraltar and ▶ to be particularly careful that it was
of good quality; and with this view to taste every

sample before concluding a bargain; he consequently tasted the quality of every cask, in every store, between the victualling-office and the dockyard, and found all so good, as always to think the last the best, till he became so tipsy, as to with difficulty scramble up the ship's side after concluding his bargain.

Captain Hallowell immediately perceiving the plight he was in, from a too scrupulous performance of the order, with respect to tasting, observed sternly, 'I am sorry to see you, Sir, set so bad an example to the boat's crew. You cannot, Sir, walk a seam of the quarter deck'; to which the reply was, 'Oh yes I can,' – 'then do it, Sir.' But five seams being found too small a space to walk in, he was consequently glad to get below, and managed to reach his berth with the assistance of the quarter-master. ◀

Dimly comprehending that the above anecdote has some connection with him, Melville Lee feels an unexpected surge of affection for the ten-year-old toper and bears with him while he danced with several young ladies at a ball for the quality of Gibraltar where Captain Hallowell met Miss Inglefield and afterwards married her. But after this, there is such a windy confusion of sailing in all directions that Melville is far more at sea than the *Swiftsure* and only regains his bearings when the fleet passed close to the Island of Stromboli where the dreadful roaring of the volcano, which sailors call "the entrance of Hell", caused someone to relate to the young sailor the story of the trial of the widow Booty.

▶ Extract from the Journal of the ship *Sphynx*, in the year 1686, up the Straits.

May 12th. – When we arrived at Manson, we found

three ships lying there from London, commanded by the Captains Bristol, Brown and Burnaby, all going to Lipari to load; on the 13th, the three ships sailed, with the *Sphynx*, (wind N.W.) to Lipari, where they anchored in twelve fathom water, (wind S.W.). The four captains and a Mr Bell, a merchant, went on shore upon the Island of Mount Stromboli, to shoot rabbits. About three o'clock they called their men together to go on board their respective ships, when to their inexpressible astonishment, they saw the appearance of two men coming very swiftly through the air towards them, — one of them appeared to be dressed in black, and the other in grey clothes. They passed close by with great rapidity, and to their extreme consternation, descended amidst the burning flames into the mouth of that dreadful volcano, Mount Stromboli. At their entrance there issued tremendous voices, the flames rushed out most terribly, and Capt. Burnaby cried out, 'Lord, bless me, — the foremost of the two in black clothes is old Mr Booty, — my next door neighbour, at Wapping, — but I do not know the other!' He then desired them all to write down in their pocket books, or note on something what they had then seen, which was immediately done by the three captains and a Mr Bell, and likewise entered in the different ship's journals at the same time. When these four ships had taken in their loading at Lipari, they sailed together for London.

When they arrived in the river Thames, at Gravesend, Capt. Burnaby's wife came from London to him. He then sent for the other three captains to come on board his ship, to congratulate him on his wife's arrival. After they had thus met, a little conversation

passed between them in the cabin, when Mrs Burnaby
suddenly started from the chair and said to her husband,
'My dear, I'll tell you some news, old Mr Booty is
dead.' He directly answered, 'We saw him go into
Hell & etc.' as before related, to her serious alarm.
When Mrs Burnaby had returned to London, she
went to an acquaintance and related this serious event,
– that her husband had seen the soul of Mr Booty go
into Hell, on the 14th of May last. This gentleman
then mentioned the same to Mrs Booty widow of the
deceased, who immediately took a writ out of the
King's Bench court, in the penal sum of one thousand
pounds damages, and arrested Captain Burnaby for
defamation of character upon her late husband's soul.
Capt. Burnaby gave bond to stand trial, and she then
took out of the court of King's Bench in Westminster
Hall summonses for all the people that had attended
the late Mr Booty in his last sickness, and at the time
of his death also. The sexton of the parish who buried
him, and the clothes he last wore before his sickness
she had taken care of, to be introduced in court, on the
day of trial. When the trial came on, the different
persons, with the black clothes were brought into
court, and were there met by Capt. Burnaby, the
captains of the other three ships, and the men of the
four boats, with Mr Bell, who were all on the said
Island of Stromboli, and saw the two apparitions
descend into the burning flames on the aforesaid 14th
day of May last.

Ten of the men of the boats made oath, that the
buttons on the coat which the apparition had on,
were like the one present, being moulds covered with
black cloth, of the same sort the coat was made of.

The different persons who were with Mr Booty at the
time of his decease made oath that his death happened
at three o'clock at noon, on the 14th day of May last,
which was in the year 1686. The jury then asked the
captain of the *Sphynx* if he knew Mr Booty in his life-
time; he answered in the affirmative, but he had never
seen him in those clothes in his life, but plainly observed the dress the apparition had on, which Mr Bell
said was Mr Booty, in company with another unknown.
The judge then spake, 'the Lord grant that I may
never see such a sight as that, – for I think it impossible
for thirty men to be mistaken.' The jury then gave
their verdict against the widow Booty – plaintiff to pay
the costs of the court.

The above trial is now to be seen on the records of
the court of King's Bench, in Westminster Hall. 'The
Mrs Booty, plaintiff, against Captain Burnaby, defen-
dant.'

The following is another extract as additional con-
firmation of Booty's trial.

It is recorded that Sir John Gresham, brother to Sir
Thomas Gresham, who built the Royal Exchange,
London, made a voyage up the Straits in King James's
reign; when he with eight of his men ascended to the
top of the burning mountain Stromboli, and there
heard a voice from the mountain proclaiming, 'Dispatch! dispatch! – for rich Antonio is coming!' When
Sir John and his men arrived at the Island of Sicily
they heard that a Mr Antonio – the richest man in that
part of the world, had died at the very time they were
upon the burning mountain, and heard the above
words issue from out of the fire of the crater. When
Sir John reached London, he, with eight of his men,

made oath before King James, to the truth of the same.

This singular relation was collected from an old manuscript in the possession of the late Lieut. W. Hunter, brother of Admiral Hunter. ◂

Here Sir T. Lee pauses and gazes solemnly at his audience who, in turn, gaze solemnly back. No one knows what to make of the prophetic mountain. In particular, Melville Lee is deeply impressed, for certain volcanic sensations in his stomach and head lead him to suppose that some innocent traveller has, at that very moment, seen him vanish tremendously into the awful mouth of the mountain.

CHAPTER FIVE
1798

In which Napoleon, temporarily abandoning the conquest of
England, dreams of an Empire in Egypt and the East, but
Nelson, divining his intention, scours the seas and, hand in
hand with Our Hero, finds the French fleet in the mouth
of the Nile – with awesome consequences.

A COLD collation has been fetched in; the passage of
dangerous years has brought the little sailor to his
early summer of 1798, and the family to lunchtime.
Dishes have been laid along the sideboard like vessels
in line of battle, and in their midst, towering high,
rocks a great meat jelly in the shape of a four-decked
man of war. Whittled carrots peep menacingly from
its ports and imprisoned fragments of mutton lurk in
the vague depths of its forecastle and poop.

Euphemia Lee cannot keep her eyes off it, and it shudders gently as if inspired with a vision of imminent defeat. Half unconsciously she lays a course through the shoals and islands and enemy frigates that abound in the room, and dreams of sinking the rich brown flagship that lies at anchor in its shallow silver tureen.

But as yet she dares not move; Papa's eyes are everywhere, scouring the room with terrible rapidity.

The French fleet had vanished from Toulon! A mighty armada carrying an army of forty thousand men, roaming the seas like an evil ghost and haunting the world with murderous expectation. Where – where was it bound?

Sir T. Lee's eyes dart from window to sideboard to door. Nothing escapes him and no one doubts that, had the French fleet been there, he would have seen it.

Once more it was moving day for nations. Like huge, sullen pike they blundered about under the stagnant surface of Europe in the wake of the brilliant dragonflies that buzzed and darted above them. Dizzily the Pitts and Napoleons performed their complicated dances, eluding each other on invisible wings of treaties and treacheries, while below, the gulping millions lumbered against each other, snapping and bleeding into the appalling dark.

The French fleet – where was it? What was to be the next figure in the dance? Urgently Lord St Vincent was ordered to detach a force from his fleet off Cadiz to search the mysterious seas. On May 24th thirteen sail of the line, with Sir Horatio Nelson at the top and Midshipman Lee somewhere nearer the bottom, set off on their enormous quest.

They reached Corsica on 12th June and Captain

Hardy of the *Mutine* went ashore for news. The French had not been seen in those waters, so the fleet sailed on and two days later stopped and boarded a Moorish vessel off the Island of Giglio. Again and again they questioned the sailors until at last they learned that the French had gone to Syracuse.

At once all sail was spread and with quickening hearts the English rushed on. Two days more brought them to the Bay of Naples and again Captain Hardy went ashore for the news the Admiral longed for. But the captain returned without it. The Ambassador, Sir William Hamilton, had seen neither stitch nor sail of the French fleet. Had it indeed been bound for Syracuse it must have coasted by Sardinia.

On June 20th the English ships sailed through the Straits of Messina; but it was in vain. There was no sign of the French fleet. To Alexandria, then — it must have gone to Alexandria; such was the size of the armada and such were the prevailing winds, that nothing else seemed possible.

With furious speed and the wind behind them, the restless searchers made for Egypt and the phantom French. On June 22nd they reached Malta and, in a rapid compact body, passed the island in blackest night, firing minute guns as they went. Such was their pace that, when dawn came, the island had vanished below the horizon.

But the island was not the only thing that had vanished in their wake. With it had gone the sight they were scouring the seas to find. At 2 a.m. they had passed within hailing distance of the silent French armada, with all its transports helpless in the night.

The English ships reached Alexandria on June

28th. The harbour was empty. Unknowingly, they had outsailed the French. Bitterly they turned about and stood towards Cyprus, for the wind continued westerly. It seemed as if the vast armada they were pursuing, the huge array of vessels that must have looked like a city under sail, was nothing but a phantom, a chimera in their Admiral's brain, to be sought and found only in a seascape of dreams.

Wearily the English hoisted sail once more for Syracuse; and on the afternoon of the day they quitted Alexandria, the huge French fleet came safely, quietly in.

The news at Syracuse was thin and vague; nothing more definite than that the French had taken Malta and steered an eastward course thereafter.

Where else but for Egypt? It *must* be Egypt. With violent haste the ships began re-victualling to continue their immense search. The task seemed endless, and in the long days of waiting, Midshipman Lee went ashore to stare at the ancient ruins, while from the harbour came the busy sounds of the men of war preparing to make new ones.

It was in Syracuse, in a solemn timeless catacomb, that antiquarian Captain Hallowell chattered engrossingly to the living friar of the place, while bright young Lee deftly broke two fingers off a dead one.

At last the ships were ready — the latter end of the task having been accomplished with supernatural speed. It was as if a ghostly monk had urged the Sicilians to prodigies of labour by holding up his reduced hand as though to say, "If their children steal fingers, what will their men take? Hurry — hurry, before we're dismantled altogether!"

On the 24th July, the English fleet left Syracuse and shaped a course for the Greek Archipelago, hoping desperately to pick up news of the phantom fleet of France; and it was off the town of Koron that the precious news was gained. Captain Troubridge, of the *Culloden*, heard from fishermen that a monstrous spread of French warships had been seen, steering south-east from Crete about a month before.

At last, at last the phantom had become a reality. The fleet bore up and sailed south-east with sails spread to catch at every breath of the wind.

▶ On the morning of the 31st a fine fresh breeze from the westward, having wafted the fleet near to the shores of Egypt, the captains of the several ships went on board the Admiral to receive his last instructions; while in the afternoon of this day, the *Swiftsure* and *Alexander* were ordered ahead to reconnoitre. At ten the following morning, (the glorious 1st of August, 1798) the Tower of Alexandria, the Pharos, and the Pillar of Pompey, met the view; but the port no longer presented the desolate aspect it did on our last visit; both the harbours being now crowded with vessels bearing the French flag, only five or six, however, were men of war . . .

At fifteen minutes past three the Admiral made the signal to prepare for battle, and the *Swiftsure* and the *Alexander* had not for more than an hour hauled up to rejoin, before they discovered the French fleet in a bay to the Eastward, anchored in line of battle; the tremendous four-decked *L'Orient* lying in the centre, with an immense French admiral's flag flying at the main; this huge ship towered like a castle over all the others around her, although some of them were 84s of the first class. All the small 74s, of which the English fleet was principally composed, appeared like frigates alongside of them; but Nelson, nothing daunted by their numbers, their weight of metal, or the strong position which they had taken up, instantly bore down to the attack.

The *Swiftsure* and *Alexander*, being thrown considerably astern by standing so far in towards the port, were now endeavouring, under a heavy press of sail, to regain their stations; the Admiral making the signal at four, to prepare to anchor with springs, and to engage as each ship came up the van and centre of the enemy's fleet. At five the *Swiftsure* was signalized to be standing into danger, upon which she hauled up and had the mortification to see the *Culloden* aground on a reef of sunken rocks extending a long way to the east from Aboukir Island, and which the fleet was not aware of, in consequence of having no chart of the place. Night was closing in when the British ships approached the enemy, who, formed in a crescent, presented a truly formidable aspect to seaward . . .

The signal was soon displayed from the mast head of the Admiral for the British line to bear up and engage that of the enemy; each ship being prepared to anchor by the stern in order to avoid the raking fire she would otherwise be exposed to, in swinging round if anchoring by the head; the cable for this purpose being carried aft along the ship's side, from the bow to the stern, and made fast to the mizen mast through one of the ports in the gun room.

The enemy's line presented a compact and formidable appearance, each ship being anchored so close that they could easily hail each other, in order to prevent the British vessels from penetrating through; while the frigates, mortar vessels, gun boats & etc. were stationed inside on the shoal that the ships of the line lay close to, and the whole supported by a cannon and mortar battery established on Aboukir Island. On Nelson viewing their position he naturally concluded, that depending upon the impossibility of the British fleet breaking through, to get between them and the land, they would therefore be unprepared for action on that side; so that by turning their line and anchoring between them and the shore, the British ships would be able to fight them on equal terms . . .

The *Goliath*, Capt. Foley, led the van, and on nearing that of the French became exposed to a heavy cannonade, which she instantly returned, and finally rounding the weathermost ship, anchored between her and the shore, on the larboard bow of the *Conquerant*, the second ship in the French line, – the remainder of the van taking up their positions in succession, between the enemy and the land . . . those following them anchoring in succession to the east of the enemy's ships engaged by the van, thereby enclosing them between two fires; *Vanguard*, Sir Horatio Nelson engaging *Spartiate Minotaur*, Capt. Thomas Louis with *Aquilon*; *Bellerophon*, Capt. Darby, alongside *L'Orient*; *Defiance*, Capt. Peyton, on bow of *Franklin*; *Majestic*, Capt. Westcott, on the quarter of *Tonnant*; and *Alexander*, Capt. Ball on the inshore quarter of *L'Orient*; the *Leander*, 50, Capt. T. B. Thompson, the last ship that entered the battle, anchoring with great judgement across the bows of the *Aquilon*, by which position she was enabled to rake the whole French line without the possibility of a return.

By the above disposition of the British squadron, the half of the French fleet were exposed to the fire of the whole British, anchored on either side of them . . .

Each British ship had been directed to hoist four lanthorns on a horizontal pole on the mizen peak as a distinguishing mark, but these being often shot away, and the night rendered still more dark by cannon smoke; consequently the *Swiftsure* and *Alexander*, which came late into action, were greatly puzzled where to take their stations – the former even being on the point of firing into the *Bellerophon*, which, dismasted and without colours or distinguishing lanthorns, was found drifting out of battle. Her position in the line was promptly taken by *Swiftsure*, but more upon *L'Orient*'s bow, whereby she was less exposed to the latter's powerful battery.

The *Spartiate*, placed between the *Vanguard* and *Theseus*, contended nobly against the double fire; the bowsprit and anchors being shot away, several ports being knocked into one, the foremast only left standing, and 410 of her men killed and wounded before submitting. The gallantry of her resistance was amply testified by the havoc made by her on board the *Vanguard* – among the sufferers being Nelson himself, who was wounded a quarter of an hour after the commencement . . .

The *Bellerophon*, intending to take a position on the bow of *L'Orient*, unfortunately did not drop anchor sufficiently soon, and consequently falling alongside her huge opponent, was obliged, in about ten minutes after anchoring by her overwhelming fire, to cut her cable and drift out of the line, totally dismasted and with the loss of 200 of her crew.

The cannonading between the rear ships of the two fleets was much more destructive than that between those of the van, the disappearance of daylight only seeming to increase the fury of the contest; the incessant flashings of the numerous guns discharged at nearly the same instant being so vivid at times as to enable each party to distinguish clearly, not only the colours of the respective combatants, but the disastrous effects of the battle upon them.

Our little Mid. being aide-de-camp to Captain Hallowell, was sent by him during the hottest period of the fight, to bring a few bottles of ginger beer from the cabin locker round the mizen mast for the refreshment of himself and other officers actively engaged on the quarter deck, and of which our little Mid. partook. Captain Hallowell, after remarking to him that the ship the *Swiftsure* was opposed to fired extremely well, turned away from the gangway where they had both hitherto stood during the whole of the action, but had not long left it before a heavy shot shivered the place to pieces, scattering the splinters for a considerable distance around.

Shortly after, Capt. Hallowell, observing an appearance of fire in the mizen chains of *L'Orient*, ordered young Lee to run below and desire Lieut. Waters, the Hon. F. Aylmer, Davis and Mudge, to point every gun that would bear upon this spot, to which also the musketry of the marines stationed on the poop under Capt. Allen, was directed, with a view of preventing the enemy from extinguishing the conflagration; and with such effective results that all their efforts to subdue it were rendered unavailing by the slaughter which the concentrated fire of the *Swiftsure* produced . . .

The brave Bruyes, the French commander in chief, having lost both his legs, was seated with tourniquets on the stumps, in an armchair facing his enemy and giving directions for extinguishing the fire, when a cannonball from the western side of the *Swiftsure*, put a period to his gallant life by nearly cutting him in two. The son of Casa Bianca, the captain of the fleet, had lost a leg and was below with the surgeon; but the father could not be prevailed upon to quit the ship even to save his own life, preferring to die beside his son rather than leave him wounded and a prey to the flames . . .

The fire soon ran up the rigging and along the yards and decks, but the honor of the French flag was nobly sustained; for although the flames obliged the people to desert their guns on the gangways and maindeck, the middle and lower decks still struggled for victory by keeping up a heavy and most destructive cannonade . . .

At this moment, when the battle raged with a fury not to be described, fourteen of the *L'Orient*'s crew, including the first Lieut. and Commissary, were taken into the lower deck ports of the *Swiftsure*, which was so near the burning *L'Orient* that the pitch ran out of her seams in streamlets down the side; the momentarily expected explosion of the immense ship beside her, causing great alarm lest she should be involved in the same awful catastrophe. Several of the seamen wished the cable to be slipped, but the brave and determined Hallowell saw, with the eye of judgement, that her present station was the best calculated to secure her from danger. The explosion would naturally throw all up into the air in the shape of an arch, and the *Swift-*

sure being, as may be supposed, near the centre thereof, consequently the greater part of the fragments would naturally be projected over and beyond her. Two sentinels were therefore placed by the cable round the mizen mast with directions to shoot anyone who might attempt to cut it; while the ports were ordered to be lowered, the magazines and hatchways closed, and every man to go under cover, provided with wet swabs and buckets of water in order to extinguish any burning fragments that might come on board during the explosion.

At this moment the scene was awfully grand; each fleet, as if by consent, had ceased from firing; the wind had fallen to a calm, from the heavy discharging of artillery, and all seemed to await in suspense the eventful moment with a feeling of anxiety indescribable.

The flames had now reached below the lower decks of the enemy's ship, but still the proud silk flag of her fallen chief seemed to float untouched amidst them. Nelson, forgetful of his own wounds, hearing from his captain of the expected fate of his rival Admiral, came on deck and ordered every boat to be dispatched to save the crew of the devoted vessel — the cold, clear, placid light of the moon formed a striking contrast with that of the burning ship, and enabled the lines of the hostile fleets to be, for the first time, clearly distinguished . . .

Every moment the dreadful explosion was expected — the least noise could now be heard where the din of war before raged with such uncontrollable violence — till at last an awful and terrific glare of light, blinding the sight, showed *L'Orient* blowing up with an astounding crash, paralyzing all around her, by which

nearly a thousand brave spirits were hastened into
eternity.

A large ignited beam fell into the foretop of the
Swiftsure and set it on fire, but the flames were soon
extinguished; other and heavier pieces bounding
against the sides or into the chains, and some even
upon the decks and booms, but all being speedily
prevented from doing mischief by the active measures
employed – the greater portion, as anticipated, passing
clear over the mastheads and falling into the sea a
considerable way beyond the tremendous explosion;
however it shook the ship more than the whole battle.
It was like an earthquake, the air rushing along the
decks and below with inconceivable violence, and
creating a tremulous motion in the ship which existed
for some minutes, and was awfully grand . . .

At 3 o'clock a.m. as daylight began to dawn, both
fleets seemed to be exhausted and the firing ceased
about four, for a short period on all sides. After this,
the *Majestic* and *Alexander* commenced firing on the
Tonnant and *Guillaume Tell* and *Generaux* and *Timoleon*
. . . At this time *L'Artimese*, French frigate of 48 guns,
having no means of escape, struck her colours; but as
the boats of the *Theseus* and other ships proceeded to
take possession, she burst into flames – her officers and
crew having previously left in their boats for the shore,
and in about half an hour she blew up. This conduct of
Capt. Estandlet, her commander, aroused the indignation of Nelson and all on board the fleet, for having
so dastardly burnt the ship after her colours had been
hauled down.

At noon on the 3rd of August, the *Timoleon* alone
remained with French colours flying . . . The captain

of the *Tonnant* had lost both his legs and knew he should not live, therefore declared he would see his vessel sink rather than surrender, unless all his crew were safely conveyed by the British to France; but on its being reported to him that *Swiftsure*, *Theseus* and *Leander* were coming down to compel him to submit . . . he reluctantly caused his colours to be lowered, dying a few hours after his ship was taken possession of by the British. The action now ceased, and the British red crossed ensign (under which, although rear-admiral Nelson was of the blue, the fleet fought in this memorable battle as more distinguishable at night), floated proudly triumphant as it had often done before over Britain's vanquished foes.

Our young Mid. was kindly permitted to go in the boat with his captain and have the gratification of being the first person of the fleet who landed on the shores of Egypt . . . The captain went up to the fort, but left our young Mid. to take care of the boat's crew — during the period of whose absence, he employed himself by picking up shells from the beach . . . ◀

He was, after all, only eleven years old.

CHAPTER SIX

1798

In which the triumphs of Napoleon are halted – in consequence of the destruction of his fleet . . . and Our Hero sees
at first hand the nature of the romantic Sheiks of Araby.

A BRILLIANT victory; perhaps the most dazzling of
all such encounters between brave ships and brave
men. Thousands floated in Aboukir Bay, saluting each
other's courage with fingers the fish had been at.

But England had been saved. Napoleon scowled,
and Pitt and his portly allies breathed so loud a sigh
of relief that the weeping of bewildered widows
seemed, by comparison, no louder than the squeaking
of harvest mice. England had been saved, and she
reeled in a summer of sunshine and roses that bloomed

with unparalleled splendour – no doubt on account of the dead in the mouth of the Nile.

Lady Lee's eyes are wide and filled with tears. Her thin hands grasp the arms of her chair as if she herself sees the sudden blazing sights of terror, agony and rage; the darkling air streaming with fragments – some of which were bleeding – and the ships, like huge cathedrals of the sea, in winding sheets of smoke, roaring and crackling heroic anthems of death. She bites on her lip as the tale of blood and death and legless men spurting in armchairs fills her with an unfamiliar anger. She dreams, wildly dreams of screaming in the bland faces of the makers of History, *What in God's name do you want with the world?*

Then the fancy passes and her stretched mind shrinks till it encompasses no more than a little boy drinking ginger beer and picking up shells by the sea. All else seems madness . . .

Admiral Nelson, with battered head but uncorrupted heart, was created a viscount; Captain Berry was knighted; and many another brave and brilliant gentleman was honoured. Unfortunately, on this occasion our young Mid. seems to have been overlooked. Though once more he'd fetched the drinks, no one thought to reward this nautical Ganymede. Perhaps they were all too busy . . .

▶ On the 10th of August, when the *Swiftsure* was nearly ready for active service, a square rigged vessel was seen standing into the bay under a crowd of sail; and as she was known to be one of the cruisers of the late French fleet, all the British ships hoisted French colours, and some French over English, as a deception. The vessel stood to within about three miles of the fleet, when appearing to suspect that all was not as it was wished to be represented, she shortened sail and hove to.

Swiftsure immediately prepared to slip, and on the Frenchman hauling off, she forthwith was under weigh, and by the evening came up with the chase which proved to be the French national corvette, *La Fortune*, commanded by Lieut. de Vassieau Citoyenne Marchaud. The prisoners were exchanged, and a surgeon, who had come on board, on hearing of the fate of his two brothers who had been blown up in *L'Orient*, appeared as if his grief knew no bounds. He threw himself on the deck on his face, and seemed to suffer so much mental agony, that all around gave him great commiseration, offering him water and all things that his deplorable situation appeared to require; but their surprise and contempt may be easily imagined when he unexpectedly sprang up like a harlequin, and slipping across to the weather side of the deck, presented to Capt. Hallowell a snuff box, begging him to take a pinch. The captain, astonished at such a harlequinade, accepted the offer out of politeness; when this person touched a secret spring and up jumped the figure of a friar – a trick that gave him inexpressible delight, but which quite disgusted Capt. Hallowell and all his officers. ◀

But Lady Lee does not altogether share her husband's and Captain Hallowell's contempt for the weird Frenchman. Dimly she perceives deeper matters in this

capering surgeon on the serious and windy deck of the
Swiftsure. She fancies him in cap and bells, with sharp
wry face peeping out of motley . . . the ancient Fool of
kings, the weary-hearted mocker of grand aspirations –
whose task it ever was to keep great men sane. Alas!
This Frenchman came too late. His office had long
since been dispensed with, for madness was in favour;
hence he was greeted with bewilderment and contempt.

What became of him, Lady Lee wonders gently.
Did he go back to his bitter task of repairing ruined
limbs and ruptured flesh for no better purpose than to
have his work come back even more terribly undone?
And did he show his comic snuff box to those who were
past repairing as the last balm his skill could administer
– the balm of laughter?

▶ Whilst laying in the bay of Aboukir, the *Swiftsure*'s
people were often employed to collect pieces of the
wreck of *L'Orient* for the ship's firewood, and fish up
small anchors to buy vegetables for the ship's company
at Rhodes, when the idea occurred to the gallant, but
at times eccentric, captain of the *Swiftsure*, to have a
coffin made for the immortal Nelson out of the main-
mast of *L'Orient*; a sufficient quantity of wood for
which was soon procured, as well as iron hoops to
make clamps for the corners; and by the joiners of the
Swiftsure a very neat coffin was made and sent the
first opportunity by Capt. Hallowell to his friend
Nelson, detailing the particulars of what it was made
from, and stating his hope, that when his triumphant
course was ended, his remains might be deposited

therein. Nelson received it as it was meant from his old and trusted friend, and always kept it in his cabin; and after the great battle of Trafalgar, his mortal remains, before lying in state at Greenwich Hospital, were, according to his often expressed desire, deposited in this coffin which he regarded as being a peculiar trophy from the most brilliant and decisive action he ever fought.

Our young Mid. often recollects getting into the coffin before it left the *Swiftsure*; and once his kind captain, by way of a joke, called to send aft the joiners to screw it up, as he meant also to send to Lord Nelson, as a present with the coffin, the youngest of those who had the honour to serve under his Lordship in this great battle. ◀

Melville Lee, listing heavily in several fathoms of claret, comes to himself – but the meeting proves hazy and insubstantial. "Youngest . . . honour to serve . . . in great battle . . ." Eerily he fancies that time has gone in a circle and they are all back at Cape St Vincent. He casts off and drifts towards his sisters, Henrietta and Sophia. He endeavours to smile encouragingly down on the portrait. Then haziness overcomes him and he seems to see the ghosts of three or four right arms coming all ways from out of his father's shoulder. He thinks he should point this out, when Henrietta's savage look briefly chills him. He goes away and Henrietta returns to her private dream of the coffin, the eccentric Captain Hallowell, and his impossible Mid. She wonders if the captain was really jesting . . . ? She shakes her head and Sophia, misunderstanding, rubs out yet another attempt to provide Sir T. Lee with a likely arm; whereupon Henrietta romantically wishes Papa had been a little more like Lord Nelson – and lost it.

For the past few minutes there has been a stealthy, but steady movement to and from the dishes on the sideboard. Emma Lee, a colourless child in faded pink, under Lady Lee's orders, plagues the dazed Melville with a plate of cold mutton; but he sheers off, smiling affectionately at his father as he goes.

Curiously enough, the stout Euphemia alone makes no move from her seat. The rich jellied flagship that had tempted her now repels her with its air of imminent and bloody destruction. She has a sensitive disposition, and when affected, the first thing to go is her appetite. She sighs, and longs for those times of balls, brightness and dashing gaiety that she feels must be a part of a sailor's life. She prefers to think of their handsome uniforms being stained with wine, not blood; and their neat, stockinged legs skipping to music, not lying tumbled under the surgeon's table . . .

Large as she is, she adores dancing, and wonders what became of that flute-playing officer, back in '95, who played his flute while Papa was sick. In her younger, more wistful way, she is as imaginative as the shapely Henrietta – though with less hope of success. It is a human tragedy that such romantic natures often reside in fat girls – and cause a grievous aching that only food can soothe. At balls and parties, what else is there for them to do but wander, in large loneliness, to the comfort of the buffet? For who will dance with a fat girl? What passionate eyes will ever gaze into

her portly twinklers – and sustain their passion? And
what manly arms are long enough – and strong
enough – to lift her up, let alone bear her away?

They say Arabs like fat girls . . . Straightway
Euphemia Lee indulges in a tiny dream of an Arab
chieftain galloping down, with arm outstretched to
catch her up and bear her off to some tented passion
in the lawless wilderness, where tender words and
tender deeds make her glad of her size. "Where did
you come from, lovely lady of the sands?" "From the
sea . . . from a ship . . ."

▶ *A cutter, standing towards the shore near the Arab's
Tower . . .* ◀ she hears her Papa say, very distantly;
and Charlotte Augusta's tireless quill scratches it
down.

"It was a cutter," she murmurs, in her Arabian
dream, and Lady Lee looks at her compassionately.
But Euphemia is deep in fancy; her fierce Arab lover
has brought her a dish of sheep's eyes. They stare up
at her with a passion she longs to requite, and she does
not know which to give herself to first, the sheik – or
the dinner.

It is not that she's entirely lost the thread of her
father's narration – indeed, dim visions of desultory
sailings and hazardous refittings in which Papa was
forever distinguishing himself and meeting the cream
of the land, float ceaselessly across her mind; but she
can never quite distinguish them from the substance
of her dreams. Similarly, her dreams tend to rise to the
bait of Papa's anecdotes, nibble at them – and then
swim deep, curiously enriched. Thus her strange
marooning and her wondrous Arab have come from
the sand hills near the tower of Mirabou, to the west

of Alexandria, where a French cutter had beached to avoid the prowling *Swiftsure* and *Emerald* . . .

▶ The crew, who were seen wandering over the sand hills on the approach of the boats, on a sudden, rushed towards the beach and made signs as if imploring protection; the cause of which was soon observed to be the approach of an armed body of Arabs, mounted and on foot. While all were anxiously observing the above from the ships, it was announced to our young Mid. that the only fresh meat dinner that could for a long time be expected was ready; but although some went below, our young sailor's anxiety to see the fate of these poor Frenchmen, far exceeded the desire to partake of the last fresh meal that was for some months to be enjoyed; and he therefore remained on deck to witness the result of this distressing occurrence.

Some of the Frenchmen were so fortunate as to be hauled off through the surf by breakers with lines attached to the boats; and even a midshipman of the *Emerald*, with a rope in his hand, jumped overboard and swam through the surf to the shore and saved, by his noble exertions, the captain and four seamen of the cutter . . . The British boats, as well as ships, approached as near the shore as possible; and indeed the *Swiftsure* and *Emerald* were scarce a mile off the beach laying to, at the time the Frenchmen were imploring to be taken on board; but it was now too late to save the majority. The Arabs had already surrounded them, and, after stripping off the clothes of the officers and men without resistance, murdered the greater part without any apparent provocation; among whom were the unfortunate general and his aide-de-camp, who, on their

knees begged for mercy; but an Arab had twice
snapped his piece at them before they both fell under
his deadly weapon.

The courier was carried into the country and there
murdered. An Arab was seen to ride off with the
dispatches . . . ◀

Mercifully, Euphemia's dreams have nibbled only the
better part of reality. Now they are fathoms below,
where no ugly piles of dead spoil their golden sands.

Not so Henrietta, whose heart is with the *Emerald*'s
brave midshipman . . . and who half wishes that Papa
had gone down to his dinner when called, and not
stayed, helplessly fascinated, to watch the hateful,
bloody scene on the sands. Such sights, she thinks, can
do little to ennoble boys of eleven . . . Then other
thoughts crowded in, not least of which is a dazed
wondering at the desperate exertions to save men who,
but a few days before, were the object of equally
desperate exertions to destroy.

CHAPTER SEVEN

1798 – 1799

In which Our Hero and the Navy maintain their blockade
of Alexandria while Napoleon, thwarted again, becomes First
Consul of the French Empire, and the all-conquering Nelson
is at last wounded to the heart at Naples by the bewitching
charms of the British Ambassador's wife – Emma Hamilton.

HAPPY England continued to rejoice in Nelson's
victory for the rest of that year; and Mr Pitt, taking
patriotic advantage of it, proposed income tax – to pay
for any further grandeur that might be coming her way.
Good God! Who would begrudge the odd shilling
towards more magnificent slaughter? Though blood
might have been cheap enough, the apparatus for
shedding it cost money . . . Pride demanded that
England should pay her way . . . even though that way
might have been curiously remote from the millions

who had to pay it. Indeed, pride made the strangest demands . . .

During the long months of the blockade of Alexandria, even the officers of the *Swiftsure* were reduced to a wretched diet: pork and rice . . . pork and rice . . . pork and rice . . .

▶Notwithstanding this, whenever a French boat with an aide-de-camp of Bonaparte came on board, the few fowls kept for the sick were dressed to give these fellows, that they might report that the English were not in want of anything . . . The English jacks, on looking over the side into the boats where the Frenchmen were dining, actually longed for some of their food which they could not demolish; a superfluity being purposely given with the view previously stated. ◀

In January 1799 a corvette from Rhodes rejoined the fleet . . . ▶but she brought from Rhodes no livestock; only wine and onions. Lieut. Davis reported that the plague was again raging in that island. Some French officers, as flags of truce, came on board to offer vegetables for the sick; but to convince them there was no want of anything, they were taken between decks and shown what order, regularity and comfort reigned there – to their utter astonishment, as they frequently expressed. These French officers dined on board, when even the poultry reserved for the sick were dressed to prove to them how well the English fared; but alas! had they known the real facts of the case, they would have been spared the expressions of surprise they used, at the sight of the comforts experienced. ◀

Sir T. Lee gazes round at his family with the liveliest pride and satisfaction as he recounts these extraordinary deeds of self-denial; and Henrietta responds by leaning past Sophia and lightly sketching a chicken leg in Papa's right hand which he appears to be waving with some defiance. She hopes the sick appreciated the sacrifices that, so to speak, had been made on their behalf. She would not like to think of them unpatriotically dying for want of their proper food. She sighs . . . and shakes her head. Alas, whenever a nation tightens its belt, it's always those below who are squashed so that those above may throw out boldly defiant chests.

Sir T. Lee falters. Something tells him his last anecdote has misfired. He feels a little bitter . . . but then reflects that womenfolk (of which he has more than his fair share) are made of softer stuff and cannot always be expected to understand the niceties of honour and manly pride. They never really see the point of it all . . . Nonetheless he changes the subject pretty quickly and remembers that the French officers, after they'd had their excellent dinner, ▸accused the English of using some extraordinary combustible fire balls, by which *L'Orient* was destroyed; and added that Bonaparte was very indignant at the British having so acted. They also said that the same balls from the gun vessels frequently set the camp on fire in the late attacks in Aboukir Bay. Mr Parr, the excellent gunner of the ship was sent for, and when asked, before these officers, whence these fire balls were obtained, with the openness and candour of that worthy man he replied, from the captured French 74 *Spartiate*. The French officers were confounded when the report was made.

The next day, our young Mid. with Capt. Hallowell
and several others, accompanied by Mr Parr, went on
shore to Nelson's Island to ascertain the effect of these
fire balls, which had obtained, from the late enquiry,
an importance not before attached to them. The first
was covered over with a white substance, and, when
set on fire, burnt most furiously, sending up volumes
of black smoke; but soon expended itself in consequence of being cut in scores all round, from each of
which the fire exuded. It was then rolled into the sea
but was not extinguished, burning with equal violence
under water as in the air till the contents were all
exhausted; continuing for more than five minutes after
this to throw up a dark black smoke to the top of the
water which had a most singular effect. A second was
set on fire, but this was of a different nature as it
almost immediately exploded; but fortunately did no
injury to the many around it. All the broken pieces
being hurled with great violence into the sea. It was
therefore thought that the fire of *L'Orient* was entirely
owing to the use of these balls by the French ships,
one of which, from the *Tonnant*, it is conjectured, fell
on board their own admiral's ship. ◀

Leaving the clouds of black, stinking smoke from
the stolen fire balls, like patriotic utterances, to obscure
the doubtful issues, Sir T. Lee sailed hastily to St Jean
d'Acre, in Syria, "to procure refreshments".

One by one, the names of places gilded by biblical
mention – Bethlehem, Jerusalem, Gethsemane – fall
devoutly from his lips, and he speaks of how he was
reminded of wondrous events and sacred deaths and
lives.

Here, the listening family hold their united breath;

they remember the damaged Friar of Syracuse, and wonder what more holy portions are to come . . . or, rather, to go.

▶ A church was shown where St John was imprisoned and beheaded; and the dungeon where his blood was shed was also exhibited. ◀

But our little Mid. makes no further mention of them. There was a convent, also, where a quantity of nuns ▶ were known to have immortalized themselves by disfiguring their persons to preserve their virtue . . . This was in the year 1291 . . . ◀ so by the time young Lee arrived, there was nothing left.

Courteously, the officers of the *Swiftsure* waited on the Pasha of St Jean d'Acre, to pay their respects.

▶ He was a very venerable old man, with a beard as white as snow . . . A short time before, having suspected the officers of his Customs of having defrauded him, he instantly put them all to death; and indeed, the appearance of several of his people who came alongside the *Swiftsure* with both eyes out, ears, nose or hands cut off, or otherwise shockingly mutilated, proved this old Pasha to be a cruel monster. ◀

Queasily, Henrietta wonders if Papa managed to lay hands on any of these more recent souvenirs, for he seems to have a deep interest in mutilation of the body while mutilation of the spirit quite passes him by.

▶ A short time before the *Swiftsure*'s arrival, *his* custom-house officers, to the number of 61, were drawn up on a sandy beach towards Mount Carmel, when the Pasha ordered his cavalry to attack them and they were instantly cut to pieces, and Turk-like, their mangled bodies left to rot in the sun . . . This old dog had lately put all his wives to death in a fit of jealousy.

The city of Acre, in a few days from this time, gained such celebrity by its gallant, almost unparalleled defence against a general and a victorious army, always used to conquer, that its name is immortalized, and also that of its cruel Pasha, who certainly deserved to be classed as brave amongst the brave. ◀

So . . . he was brave, thinks Lady Lee, looking steadfastly down at her pale hands which are clenched in her gown. And that covers all. They were all so brave: the ships' captains, who, blasted and torn almost to life's extinction, still fought heroically to the last drop of their crews' blood. What kind of a blanket must this bravery have been that obscured everything save the gaudy gates of a famous grave?

Sadly she feels she lacks some nobler vision. Her notion of bravery is so much smaller than her husband's. She thought the young Mid. had been truly brave during a frightful storm when the *Swiftsure* had been driven near the dangerous rocks of Crete.

▶ The young Mid. recollects that he then felt so certain a short time would terminate all their hopes and fears that he went below and liberated two doves and a hawk which he had brought from Cyprus . . .◀

It was a pity, she sighs, that no one saw fit to give him a medal or a little dirk for this one act that showed he still owned the capacity to think beyond himself, even when desperate with fear.

So strange is Lady Lee's notion of bravery that she is more stirred by a small boy's freeing his pet birds so they might escape the fate that threatened him, than by all the mutilated heroics of the captains and Pashas put together.

At last, on the 20th of March, creaking and battle weary, the *Swiftsure* came to Palermo, where the *Foudroyant*, with Admiral Lord Nelson's flag, was lying.

▶ The beautiful objects to be seen at Palermo render this interesting city second only to Naples . . . The Capuchin monastery here is well worth inspecting, on account of its containing a cemetery where the dead bodies of the nobility, monks &c. as already described at Syracuse, are deposited, tied up in their gayest attire in separate niches in the walls — ◀

"No!" breathes Henrietta involuntarily. "Oh no!" Sir T. Lee looks at her inquiringly; then, misunderstanding, explains that, ▶ The bodies are regularly prepared in an oven, where all moisture is thoroughly dried out before they are considered in a fit state to be dressed in their intended habiliments and placed in their destined niche in the wall of the cemetery. ◀

Briefly he fumbles in his pocket, but to everyone's relief he brings out no other hand than his own, holding a handkerchief. He wipes his lips and then goes on with a singularly agreeable memory . . .

▶ The principal inhabitants have splendid palaces without the walls of the city, one of which was occupied by Sir William Hamilton, the British Ambassador, where Lord Nelson lived; and there the young Mid. had the honour to wait on his lordship . . . The gallant admiral introduced the old veteran, as he termed the young sailor, to Lady Hamilton, who kindly invited him to dinner, and to a ball the same evening, which he most gratefully accepted and went on board to get rigged for such a joyous occasion; as he was never so delighted as when in the presence of, and noticed – as he always was most kindly – by his beloved and honored Admiral, Nelson. Lady Hamilton did him the honor to dance with him, and made him sleep at the palace and take breakfast with Sir William Hamilton and Lord Nelson before going on board . . .

Captain Hallowell, on the 27th of March, gave a ball and supper to Sir Wm. Hamilton, the British Ambassador, Lady Hamilton, Lord Nelson, several of the nobility of Palermo and the principal officers of H.M. ships then in the bay. The quarter deck, as was usual on Capt. Hallowell giving these entertainments (of which he was very fond), was tastefully hung round with all the flags of the nations then in amity with Great Britain; and on this occasion that of Naples and England were entwined with great taste. The dancing was on the quarter deck, the poop was for cards; an elegant refreshment afterwards followed, and all were delighted with the novelty and gaiety of this lively and interesting scene; and daylight had long peeped through the different flags on the mazy dancers before the company departed. ◀

Melville Lee, feeling decidedly mazy himself, weaves uncertainly towards the door, thinking to follow the company's example; but he is headed off by the sideboard. He smiles feebly and leans back, resting his elbow in the meat jelly.

But Euphemia Lee is in Heaven at last. In her mind's eye, she capers the looped deck and her fat little feet thud a sweet tattoo on the shifting boards. The flags flutter, the band plays, and the lamplit night charms the tasselled sailors' sight so that flagships seem like dainty frigates and the portly maiden no more than a nymph with a large shadow; nothing is for certain save the languorous gleaming of eyes. Her appetite returns and she glides across to the sideboard like a bulky crimson ghost to haunt the remains of the meat jelly . . .

Sourly Henrietta watches her fat sister go – and wonders that she can be so insensitive. Euphemia's glazed dreaminess repels her and she marvels that they can be of the same blood. Nelson and Emma Hamilton. How is it possible to smile and eat like a pig when such names still hang in the air? Henrietta could weep. Under her sharpness and humour lies a deep, often burning passion, and the great Admiral's love for the Ambassador's lady has ever been the peak of her dreaming. Now a painful bitterness fills her. The scene presented by Papa of Lady Hamilton and Lord Nelson has been so ordinarily amiable . . . even to the extent of that marvellous *she* dancing with ogling little Lee – like an aunt at a birthday party. Oh God! was even *their* grand passion so – so commonplace? How could they be in the same room without flying into each other's arms? How could they *exist* in the stifling company of – of "our young Mid."?

Furiously Henrietta stares at the unfinished portrait of Sir T. Lee whose whole life seems to be a denial of the high romantic spirit. It is such as he who drags the world down to dreadful everyday! With misted eyes she glances towards her mother, with whom she had always been close and shared many unspoken dreams.

But Lady Lee is smiling into the phantom air as if
she is deeply moved that so grand a passion and so
great a love could have been generous enough to be
commonplace in a common place . . .

CHAPTER EIGHT
1798 — 1802

In which Our Hero, leaving the Mediterranean in stout
hands, goes home — and Napoleon promptly wins fresh
victories across the flimsy map of Europe. But Nelson's
victory still lingers on and the French capitulate in Egypt;
then in 1801 the great admiral (without the assistance of
Our Hero) blasts the Danes out of the sea at Copenhagen.

THE little sailor was going home. The time had come
for the child-o'-war to return to his home port — for
refitting, so to speak — to undergo the prescribed
studies at the Naval Academy that he might fly a
lieutenant's flag at his mast head.

▶ This day, the last the young sailor was to spend
at Palermo, Lord Nelson went to visit the King of the
Two Sicilies . . . The King and Queen were very
familiar and spoke to Lord Nelson as an old friend
with the greatest apparent intimacy . . . ◀

Sadly the little midshipman bade farewell to the glittering scene, pricking down each separate bright aspect like a jeweller's pattern in his brain. Here was the very yardstick of greatness and success – to be familiar with queens and kings.

The great Admiral smiled and obtained a passage for him aboard the *Bulldog*, bound for Gibraltar, and placed him under the care of Captain Adam Drummond. Captain Drummond? Yes, indeed . . . "Captain (now the present Admiral) Drummond who, a few years after, married Lady Charlotte Menzies, the eldest daughter of the Duke of Athol, from whom he experienced very great kindness which he can never forget, and the friendship thus begun has been continued through life."

Nelson might have had his kings and queens; but John Theophilus Lee had his sons-in-law of dukes.

To Gibraltar, then, and there to meet with the immortal Earl St Vincent who turned sufficiently mortal at the sight of the homeward bound child to unbend and ask him if he was "low in cash", to which the answer was, ▶"Nearly aground, my Lord." "I expected as much; well boy, I will set you afloat; come and dine with me today." "Thank you, my Lord"; and with a low bow the Mid. made sail from the admiral . . .

On going towards the Spanish church, his old friend Prealdi, an élève of Lord Nelson's and a son of the general of that name, the late governor of Corsica, was discovered. They shook hands most cordially, and then taking each other by the arm, rolled down the main street of Gibraltar, greater men than the admiral

in their own estimation. Prealdi questioned his friend
whether he had received some prize money for *Aurora*,
then due at Ross and Co's, naval agents at Gibraltar;
and finding that one hundred dollars were payable to
the young Mid. thither they both repaired, the prize
book being signed and the Mid.'s share handed over
to him, both these hopeful sailors then proceeded on
their way in great glee at such a lucky hit.

The first hatter's shop was entered and a fine gold
laced cocked hat purchased for £6 sterling by the new-
comer; Prealdi already having one of these enviable
hats; for in those days Mids. as well as Admirals wore
them, – not so now. ◀

"Not so now . . ." The words were half whispered and
Sir T. Lee's eyes mist over as the scene floods his inner
sight . . . Gay, reckless Prealdi and he, high on a
mountain of childhood, wearing their admirals' hats
like a pair of snuffers, but from under which peeped
inextinguishable eyes. Oh Lord! was it really so?
Where are we now? He blinks, for gay Prealdi was shot
through the head when he was just sixteen . . .

They went to the Ordnance Arms and drank porter
till the wit fairly bubbled out of them. Sir T. Lee
attempts to evoke a sample of it, and stumbles through
a lengthy anecdote of empty bottles and soldiers and
military officers and devastating replies, delivered with
sang-froid. It is neither funny nor witty – but doubtless it was at the time; everyone laughs – for it would
have been very cruel not to.

Six young and cheerful weeks he spent in Gibraltar,
and then, one day, he was told that the *Childers* brig
was to sail that evening for England and he was to

embark at once. ▶ With deep regret he took an affectionate and long farewell of his friend, Prealdi, whom he was destined never more to behold . . . Ever will our narrator revere his memory. ◀

Sir T. Lee blinks furiously as uncanny tears topple out of his eyes like a sudden heavy dew after a long night. He shifts his arm as if he feels again Prealdi's eager young hand grasping it to lead him rolling down the narrow hot streets of Gibraltar towards the Ordnance Arms . . . For better or worse, this was the end of his childhood; and his tears are as much for himself as for lively, witty, wonderful Prealdi.

▶ The *Childers* did not meet with anything worthy of notice till her arrival at Plymouth after a passage of twenty days. The brig came to anchor between the island and the main to perform quarantine for 14 days, and the most tedious fortnight it proved . . . Every day did the narrator look for hours with a glass to see if he could recognize, among the numerous promenaders who came of the Hoe at Plymouth, any one with whom he was acquainted. At last the day of deliverance arrived, the yellow flag was hauled down and in less than half an hour the young Mid. took leave of his kind commander, and landed . . . He was impatient to a degree to see his beloved mother and sister . . . ◀

But on the very day that he'd arrived in England, an old and respected acquaintance had called on his home in Tamerton, an acquaintance he must have thought he'd left behind him, at sea. Death. His sister had died.

He met his mother by the church, with a party of relations; but she ▶ did not know him, not expecting his return, and indeed if he were even alive, as she had not heard from him for nine months before; and therefore passed on. He jumped off his horse and ran into the churchyard and through it so quickly that he met the whole party at the opposite gate through which they had to pass, when he sprang forward into his mother's arms . . . ◄

So the homecoming was muted; the death of his sister sharpened every familiar sight in the house and village till it became a piercing memory of grief and loss beyond the bewildered mother's enduring.

They moved away into Cornwall, and there they stayed till the shore-bound Midshipman was ordered to begin his studies at the Royal Academy at Portsmouth.

But the old familiar acquaintance was not so easily avoided. It was as if in the little sailor he'd found a small, but respectful friend. Captain Lee, coming home from the Cape of Good Hope, caught cold at Greenwich, and, in spite of active bleeding, in three days sank like a stone. ▶ His remains were deposited in the Mausoleum of Greenwich Hospital with all the honors of a military funeral, attended by all his ship's company, by whom he was greatly beloved; as was evinced by their orderly conduct as well as by each man providing at his own expense a piece of crape to wear around his arm on the occasion, and which they continued to wear for weeks after. The officers and a certain number of the pensioners of Greenwich hospital also attended, and the pall was borne by four admirals and two captains of the navy. ◄

Sir T. Lee falls briefly silent as he bequeaths this

memory of Grandpapa's stately entombment. Nothing confers honour like death. Throughout his life it has seemed like a seal of quality.

It has always been a comfortable thought and has perhaps helped him to survive the mutilating slaughter that seasoned his childhood – and to become the well-regulated gentleman he now is.

CHAPTER NINE

1802 – 1805

In which Napoleon secures a brief peace with England – then
strikes again; but Our Hero is ready for him and takes his
position at the helm of an Admiralty desk. So Nelson goes
alone to Trafalgar – and does not come back.

So John Theophilus Lee plunged himself deep into
nautical studies while over his head the world rolled on
uproariously. Your Austrias, Brunswicks, Denmarks,
Two Sicilies, and all the rest of the gaudy raggle-taggle
performed their complicated dances to the grand old
tune of cannons, screams and widows' tears.

Countries were being saved, countries were being
lost – and everywhere great and patriotic men were
roaring and raving at their countryfolk to "Stand
firm!", "Defend the homeland!" and "Fight for
Freedom!" till the bewildered listeners actually came

to believe that chains stamped "foreign made" were of a more constricting fit than those that had been forged at home. So they obliged and fought with a violence that was extraordinary, butchering each other on land and sea and in the once sweet rivers, while their kings and ministers sweated with excitement and cried spitefully at one another, "Take that!"

And then – and then, in 1802, there was peace. Everything stopped. It was as if it had all been a dreadful misunderstanding. Came a tremendous and joyful shaking of hands – and an ocean of mutual regard. Doubtless, deep underground, the tens of thousands of massacred husbands and fathers spat the worms out of their mouths and begged each other's pardons for having behaved so uncivilly – for look! those they'd bravely followed were now the choicest of friends! Not even in their secret prayers did those architects of wholesale death apologize for still being alive. There is no guilt in politicians; a madness drives it out.

Then in 1803, England, in a manner of speaking, woke up again. Every blade of grass, so to speak, stood bolt upright, and every hedgerow flower opened wide its eyes. Bonaparte was a monster; England was in dreadful peril yet again. The very oaks shuddered, and no right-thinking gentlemen could walk in his park without hearing every single bird sing piteously, "Save me from Napoleon!"

Fortunately, those who didn't hear such urgent, natural cries had no voice in the affairs of the nation; nevertheless, their deafness, poverty and ignorance was not held against them and they were given every opportunity of returning to the glorious slaughter. There is

no limit to the generosity of patriots with their countrymen's blood.

▸About this period, our young Mid. having finished
his studies and that fine frigate, *La Minerve*, lying at
Spithead, commanded by his old shipmate and gallant
friend, Capt. Jahleel Brenton, he forthwith made appli-
cation to the Admiralty for his appointment to that
ship . . . and our young Mid. once more embarked on
his favorite element, rather against the inclination of
his dear mother . . .

Luxuries had now begun to be introduced into the
midshipman's berth; – a couple of casks of wine in
slings, and sheep and poultry constituting part of the
mess stock; articles unknown in a midshipman's berth
in former times.

The young Mid. and one of his messmates, Jackson
Pearson, the son of Sir Richard Pearson, being both
desirous of visiting their parents at Greenwich, Capt.
Brenton did not think it wise that these two young lads
should go together lest by some wild tricks they might
get into scrapes, so therefore desired them to toss up a
piece of money to determine who should go first. The
chance was tried and the narrator lost; his friend and
messmate therefore proceeded to Greenwich without
him, to his great chagrin; as he was most desirous of
going first; but how good and gracious was Almighty
Providence towards him. The leave expired, Pearson
returned and the young sailor met him at the Three
Kings Tavern in Deal, and that night set off for
Greenwich.

Arrived at Greenwich, he found his dear and anxious
mother ready to receive him. Letters of Marque had

been issued against France and war was inevitable. The
day had just arrived for the Mid.'s return to his ship;
when . . . he met his old and much respected friend,
Admiral John Hunter, who said, 'What a lucky fellow
you are to be here. Do you know that your ship is
wrecked and captured off Cherbourg, and all surviving
hands made prisoners after a loss of many killed and
wounded?' This was at the commencement of the war
when Bonaparte refused to exchange prisoners with the
English and La Minerve's crew and officers were, in
consequence, detained 13 or 14 years in the several
fortresses of Bische, Besancor &c. The young Mid.
was thunderstruck . . . and he then felt how much
reason he had to be thankful to divine Providence . . . ◀

Thus he made the discovery that divine Providence is
as concerned with a single midshipman as with the
course of nations; perhaps more so . . . As further
evidence, it happened on the very next day at Greenwich Hospital that an old friend of his father's offered
him a post in a public board under the Admiralty. Lord
Hood, the Governor of Greenwich Hospital, shrewdly
advised acceptance. But Lord St Vincent – who had
once had a man hanged for a third mug of water –
sternly advised against it. His mother pleaded for it.
He wavered. The noble Lord St Vincent took offence
and wrote to the mother saying that, ▶ The kind and
tender feelings of a mother would continue to the ruin
of her son; that the young sailor's prospects in the naval
line were such as would be courted by the first families
in the kingdom; and that if he did not go to the West
Indies with the commission offered, he would mar all

that had heretofore been done for him in the naval service. ◀

On which Mrs Lee became quite ill. The young midshipman was in a quandary as these great forces battled for his innocent young soul. What was his course to be? Should he accept the patronage of the immortal Earl — or the patronage of Divine Providence? Though his whole nature recoiled from the idea of rejecting the assistance of a noble lord on one side, there was, on the other side, another.

He accepted the civil appointment and declined to go abroad. Providence, his mother, Lord Hood, and the old friend (who happened to be the chairman of the public board in question), had won. The immortal Earl St Vincent, ungenerous in defeat, declared he'd never see him more; but after three years he changed his mind . . .

▶ Our narrator's kind friend, Lord Nelson, did not feel so indignant at his leaving the navy; his Lordship called on him two days before he left town, in 1805, and expressing himself happy to find he was so comfortably situated, asked him to walk with him down the Strand as far as Salter's shop, which he was proud to do. The crowd, which waited outside Somerset House till the noble viscount came out, was very great. He was then very ill and neither in look nor dress betokened the naval hero, having on a pair of drab-green breeches, and high black gaiters, a yellow waistcoat, and a plain blue coat with a cocked hat, quite square, a large green shade over the eye and a gold headed stick in his hand; yet the crowd ran before him and said, as he looked down, that he was then thinking of burning a fleet &c. They gave his lordship repeated and hearty cheers;

indeed the two pedestrians could hardly get to Salter's shop, so dense was the crowd. Lord Nelson said to our narrator, "Does not this remind you of former days at Naples, when the crowd thus pressed upon me?" On arriving at Salter's shop, the door was closed and his Lordship inspected all his swords which had been presented at different periods, with the diamond aigrette, numerous snuff boxes &c. Sir Thomas Thompson came in at this moment, and appearing to have something to say in private to the noble Lord, our narrator received a kind and hearty shake by the hand from the Hero of the Nile; and then withdrew, highly gratified at the honor his lordship had done him in calling on him when so much otherwise engaged. Lord Nelson said during the conversation they had before Sir Thomas Thompson came in, "I have still the coffin which that good fellow Hallowell made for me on board your ship," adding, "I always keep it in my cabin." ◀

Strange meeting . . . and yet not so strange. The great Admiral, ill and tormented by many opposing aspirations and emotions, must have thought often of death, and so of the curious gift of Captain Hallowell. Perhaps, of late, the grim shape of it had been much before his inner eye . . . And Naples after the Nile. That too must have been in his thoughts . . . Emma in those days, under the lanterns of the *Swiftsure*'s quarter deck; laughing and dancing with that bright-eyed child . . . Lee, that was it . . . little Lee . . . the *Swiftsure* . . . Hallowell and the coffin. Little Lee watching him everywhere, drinking him in, memorizing every line of his face, every vein in his hand – as if to tell his unborn

children and make Lord Nelson live again. Lee . . .
John Lee. Hallowell said he often climbed into the
coffin . . . its first inhabitant; and yet he danced with
Emma . . . a child . . . Where is he now?

So he found him out — and was not at all indignant
that he'd left the navy. The troubled admiral, half-
weary with life, saw much more clearly into the young
man than had the stern St Vincent.

Such as Lee were the spectators of history, the con-
noisseurs of memories into whose collections great
men, whether they liked it or no, were fated to go.

CHAPTER TEN

1806 – 1814

In which Mr Pitt dies and Our Hero marries. Napoleon invades Spain but the Duke of Wellington, also connected by marriage to Our Hero, stands against him and halts his progress. Napoleon invades Russia and his empire reaches its highest point. Our Hero plays golf, and Napoleon's empire begins to topple.

A CONNOISSEUR of memories, a discriminating collector, so to speak. But not a creator. The genius was different. He had taste instead of ability; it is not possible to have both. Thus gentlemen who collect handsome paintings do not paint themselves. Taste prevents it; to set what they could do beside what they could buy would be desperate.

John Theophilus Lee, who'd been given every opportunity of producing masterpieces of heroics in a pair of gigantic battles, had only managed to fetch

watered wine in the one and ginger beer in the other —
neither of which were striking pigments. But on the
other hand, he'd danced with Emma Hamilton and
shaken Lord Nelson's hand. He was a collector, and a
wonderfully astute one. So perhaps sensing his talent,
he went his way, picking and choosing, at the ceaseless
auctions of events, just those items he longed to
possess.

He specialized — as your true collector must; he
specialized in European nobility. No search was too
arduous, no effort too humiliating to button-hole the
elusive Lord or the rare Duke. Not Napoleon himself
in his quest for glory was as single-minded as was John
Theophilus Lee in his quest to shake hands with it.

In 1806 he picked up an astonishing bargain at the
Blackheath Golf Club — of which he was a member.
There, ▶through Mr Charles Broughton and Mr
Ruperti he became intimate with the late reigning
Duke of Brunswick (brother to Queen Caroline)◀.

Your golf clubs are first-rate places for picking up
the unexpected treasure . . . which, in part, explains the
popularity of the game. Though all men may be equal
on the green, your shrewd collector will always be able
to distinguish between the rubbish and the treasure
and, smiling slyly, bear it off . . .

▶This amiable man used often, with his two sons,
the late and present reigning Duke of Brunswick, to
visit the narrator at Greenwich; and always honored
him by partaking of the cold collation of the Blackheath
Golf Club . . . The kind-hearted Duke of Brunswick
seemed to enter into the pleasures of this old Scottish
game and frequently brought his sister, the Princess of
Wales . . . and always made a point of attending the

grand anniversary dinner at the Green Man, Blackheath . . .

The illustrious Duke was with our narrator for
several hours the day that he left this country for the
last time. Little was it then expected that in three short
weeks . . . he would fall gloriously, at Quatre Bras, at
the head of his own troops . . . at the commencement of
the great Battle of Waterloo. ◀

Sir T. Lee's voice has become oddly resonant, and
seems to echo in the room. The afternoon shadows
have deepened, and the corners of the room have
become indistinct. Henrietta Lee gazes from one to
another, fancying at times that she sees in them the
ghost of the old Duke – whom she dimly remembers
as a phantom of whiskers and stars, smelling of gun-
powdery perfume and snuff.

How curious, how very curious, that, like the glorious Nelson before him, the ill-fated Duke should have
chosen Papa to visit before embarking on his last
adventure. What is it about this sharp-eyed, but not
very important gentleman that brings the great ones
in their bright courses drifting his way? Almighty
Providence – or an obscure feeling that all their greatness is an illusion unless bequeathed to such as Sir T.
Lee? For, in a way, he is real and they are dreams. He
gives them substance, and grandeur. He keeps them
bright and shows them off; and he keeps them only in
the very best company. Without Sir T. Lee they would
have been no better than the common dead; the aristoc-
racy of power would crumble and leaders go shuddering
into the grave to face the hatred of those they'd led –
with no defence left in the world against it.

Suddenly, this odd notion of Papa as the connoisseur
explains something that has always puzzled Henrietta –
and, indeed, Sophia as well. With delighted under-
standing, she nods and smiles as Sir T. Lee relates that,
▶ Still living at Greenwich, our narrator in 1807
married when only twenty years of age, Miss Sophia
Lawlor, the youngest daughter of Major Lawlor of
Thornton Place. ◀

Often, Henrietta and Sophia had wondered why
Papa had married a plain Major's daughter with not
even an Hon. to bless herself with. As far as they knew,
Miss Lawlor's fortune had not been tremendous – so
they'd concluded an overmastering passion had been
to blame. But in their heart of hearts, neither of the
sisters had been altogether convinced. A little love,
yes; but a great burning mountain of it, never!
Henrietta's notions of high romance could never admit
Papa to the realms of deathless love; so there had
always been a mystery about the union.

But now Henrietta understood. For Papa to have
made love to a Duke's daughter or a Baron's niece
would have been grotesque. It would have seemed
to him like painting rouge and face patches on a
Raphael Madonna . . . Respect for his fine collection
was a deep part of Sir T. Lee's nature; and it was out
of the question for him to respect anyone he married.
So a little love – and a little money – had been quite
sufficient . . .

Compassionately Henrietta glances at her mother.
Lady Lee catches her daughter's eye; and faintly
smiles. The name, Sophia Lawlor, falling on the air,
stirs bright memories. She remembers a nautical young
man swaggering across her young life and bewitching

it with wild, brave tales. Lord above! a sailor! There
had indeed been a little love . . .

▶ He was speedily gifted, in 1808, with his eldest son,
whom he named Horatio Nelson, after his dear and
lamented friend; as the great Nelson always told him
to call his eldest son, if he ever had one, after him and
he would be his god-father. ◀

But alas! this "fine and promising boy" went pre-
maturely to claim his great namesake's acquaintance.
Becoming a sailor, he went to South America under the
flag of Sir Thomas Hardy. There he boarded a slave
ship, caught a fever and died. ▶ His remains were interred in the British burial ground at Bahia, attended
by the commander in chief, the amiable Sir Thomas
Hardy and all the officers of the ships then in port.

A marble monument has since been sent out by his
father to commemorate the spot where Horatio Lee
and one of his young messmates, Ogilvie, a nephew of
Admiral Sir William Hope, who caught the fever from
him, lay side by side. It is astonishing how many
friends this youth had made. One of them, Lord
William Paget, a warm-hearted creature, waited and
painted all the letters cut in a head board at first
erected over his grave; and his distressed father received no less than ten letters from individuals, perfectly unknown to him, condoling with and detailing
some gratifying anecdote of the lamented youth. ◀

If ever poets and philosophers are confounded, it is
by Sir T. Lee who, riding roughshod over such harsh
notions as Caesar's dust stopping up a bung hole, shows
that burial levels, not down, but up. Though he loved
his son and truly grieved at his loss, he felt that the lad

had done well for himself. As he had been fated to die, he had made the most of it and done it in unexceptionable company. When all was said and done, where else might a Lee lie side by side with Sir William Hope's nephew save in the grave? And why else might a warm-hearted creature like Lord William Paget paint his name on a head board with his own hand but to mark the melancholy spot? One cannot have it both ways . . .

Here he broods for a moment on the hurly-burly of life and the dignity of death; then he bids Charlotte Augusta to strike out "warm-hearted creature" and put in "amiable man". One does not call a nobleman warm-hearted.

▶About two years after his marriage, the narrator had the inexpressible grief to lose his dear, his much loved mother, who breathed her last in his arms. This best of beings was interred with his father in the mausoleum in Greenwich Hospital. ◀

At this, Lady Lee looks genuinely sad. She is very sorry indeed that her mother-in-law is dead. Considering her husband's attitude to the deceased, his mother dead is altogether a more formidable lady than ever she was alive.

▶Successively our narrator had born to him twelve children; the second being a son named after himself, and then a dear, interesting girl Henrietta, with another sweet, amiable girl named Sophia, – these two girls with three others, Emma, Augusta and Euphemia are now the pride and solace of his life; – indeed, never was man more blessed with his children. He has also two fine boys, Melville and Alfred (from whose talents he expects much). He lost in 1830, by the scarlet fever, three of the sweetest little children that were ever seen, – Marion, aged 7 years, Georgina, 5 years, and Paget, 4 years, all in the space of fourteen days. ◀

One by one as he names them, he nods them, smiling, into existence; and then, irretrievably far above their heads, he nods to Marion, Georgina and Paget, now more beautiful than ever.

Then his eyes descend to the sideboard where the remains of the cold collation lie mournfully tumbled in the dishes, like some rich old graveyard sleeping in silver grass. Against the edge of the sideboard leans his eldest surviving son, John, in a mirror image of his own easy attitude. For a moment John smiles feebly at his father; then he drops his eyes. He is no Horatio – and he and his father know it. In Sir T. Lee's affections, there is no rivalling the dead. He goes on . . .

An odd thing has begun to happen. Everyone – save Melville Lee who is in a world of his own and struggling with it – stares sharply at Charlotte Augusta. So long quiet, so long industrious, so long scholarly in her gauzy gown and with her busy quill . . . and now giggling helplessly! She is shaking like some tremendous and unseasonable butterfly.

Lady Lee shakes her head as Sir T. Lee seems about to ask the reason. It will only make her worse, she indicates, if you pay too much attention. So Sir T. Lee continues doubtfully, and wonders how much of his Memoir is being lost in the intermittent quakings of Charlotte Augusta's quill. He suspects she is giggling at the wretched Melville who still has meat jelly dripping from his sleeve. He cannot see what else could be amusing her. Nor, for that matter, can anyone else understand why the ordinarily studious Charlotte Augusta is convulsed with mirth.

▶Not long after he entered the civil service, the mode of supplying lemon juice for the navy occurred to him as very injudicious and expensive; nine shillings and sixpence per gallon being paid for it in London, while he knew that at Messina the British Consul could contract for fifty or a hundred thousand gallons of fresh squeezed juice at a time for one shilling and three-pence per gallon, free from all deleterious ingredients with which the other was known to be adulterated.◀

The tears are gushing from Charlotte Augusta's eyes and she's forced to stop writing in order to wipe them away. She catches Henrietta's puzzled look and tries to indicate what she's written down; then she's off again and has to bite her lip savagely to prevent an outward explosion.

▶By this plan in war time £20,000 sterling per annum was saved. All the lemon juice in the naval service has ever since been obtained from a Mr Thurban of Messina.◀

It's no use. Charlotte Augusta has to stop. She cannot go on. Laughter keeps rising within her like a tidal wave. Fiercely she attempts to fix her thoughts on St Sebastian and all the Christian martyrs to stop herself from laughing. But – but it's no good. Lemon juice! Oh – oh Papa! Drinks again . . . watered wine at St Vincent . . . ginger beer at the Nile, and now – oh Papa! You've done it again! Lemon juice for *everyone*! A wholesale Ganymede – Papa!

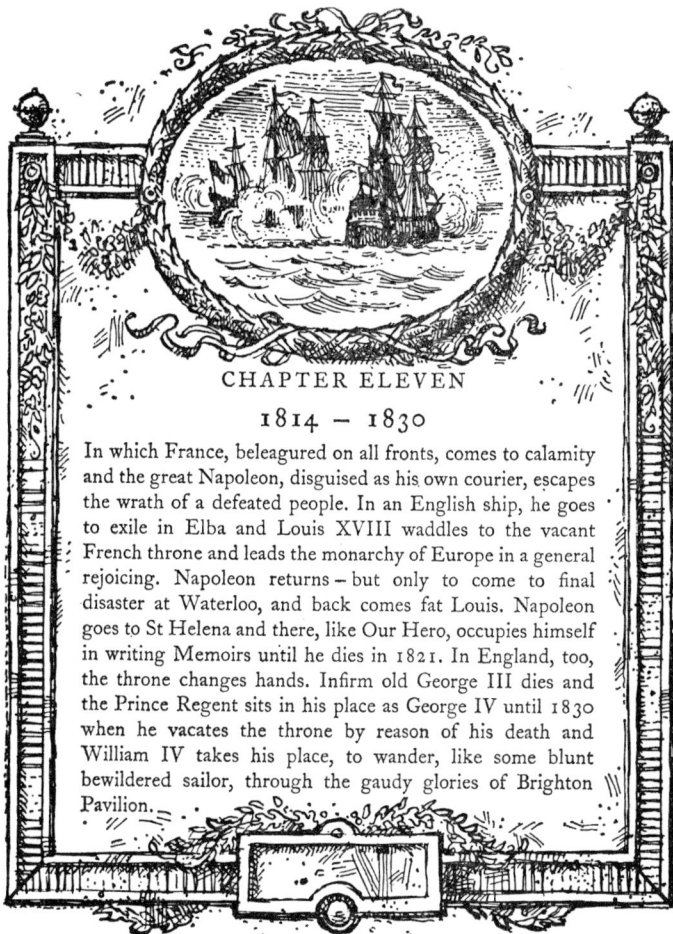

CHAPTER ELEVEN
1814 — 1830

In which France, beleagured on all fronts, comes to calamity and the great Napoleon, disguised as his own courier, escapes the wrath of a defeated people. In an English ship, he goes to exile in Elba and Louis XVIII waddles to the vacant French throne and leads the monarchy of Europe in a general rejoicing. Napoleon returns – but only to come to final disaster at Waterloo, and back comes fat Louis. Napoleon goes to St Helena and there, like Our Hero, occupies himself in writing Memoirs until he dies in 1821. In England, too, the throne changes hands. Infirm old George III dies and the Prince Regent sits in his place as George IV until 1830 when he vacates the throne by reason of his death and William IV takes his place, to wander, like some blunt bewildered sailor, through the gaudy glories of Brighton Pavilion.

CHARLOTTE AUGUSTA has recovered now and is serious again. Candles have been lit, and dead dukes and shadows chased from the corners to flicker and scamper across the crowded floor. Lady Lee, staring out of the window towards the wide romantic sea, is distracted by the reflection of the brightened room.

It seems to fill all the world; her children lean and lounge in the streaky sky and, high in their midst, rises Sir T. Lee himself, monarch of the candlelit clouds.

The monster Bonaparte straddled the universe; Europe was in chains. From the embattled cliffs of Dover, on a clear day, you could hear them, jingling faintly in the distance. Or was it only the sound of stars and medals on fat archdukes as they scuttled – with their ruttish families – in search of someone to help them back into their gaudy jobs? England alone stood against the tyrant – and her statesmen, generals and admirals defiantly made a million widows to get the fat men back to comfort. Meanwhile . . .

▶ On the 14th of February in every year (Valentine's day), a visit to Rochetts for a week was always undertaken, and at this princely establishment with his late noble chief the Earl St Vincent, time was always agreeably spent; at the table of his distinguished host were invariably gathered many of the first men in the kingdom. The veteran Earl, although then near 75 years of age, always rose at 4 o'clock, winter or summer, and having perused and answered all his letters, was ever the first in the breakfast room, stored with all the news of the day. ◀

The news of the day. The stern old man, as he listened to the first men of the kingdom eagerly relating their tales of crimson glory, must have wept to have been out of it all . . . and cursed his years. His only comfort must have been in such as Sir T. Lee who always could be relied on to keep his grandeur bright and shining even in this winter of age. So the ancient hero lingered on, like some tinsel ghost in his huge mansion, rising at 4 o'clock – perhaps with other ghosts too, some headless, some legless, some in so many separate parts that the gun deck of a flagship might have been carpeted with them . . . and one in particular with a muslin bag over his head and a handkerchief in his hand that he could not drop . . . Give the signal, Patrick McCrink, to be strangled . . . Then must the withered Earl have longed for Valentine's day to come again!

▶ At the end of the week the narrator reluctantly left his kind, noble friend with a promise given to return again . . .

The narrator was now living at Greenwich . . . and, after being but a very few years in office, was advanced over the heads of nearly thirty, and placed in control of a large department. Shortly after this, peace was brought about by the downfall of the great Napoleon. ◀

Here, Sir T. Lee pauses with an expression of gratified surprise. It has never occurred to him before how closely the one event followed on the other; but he is too modest to suggest a definite connection between Napoleon's defeat and his own advancement. Nonetheless . . . ?

At last it had come about that the fat men were to get their jobs back; and in a tinkling ecstasy of gratitude they waddled to thank the heroic island for having taken so much trouble . . .

▶ It was indeed an unprecedented event for the Czar of Russia, the sovereign of Prussia and all the principal statesmen of Europe thus to pay their homage of admiration to the ruler and people of Great Britain. ◀

Jervis at St Vincent, Nelson at the Nile, and Napoleon at Austerlitz must have felt something of the excitement and exhilaration that Sir T. Lee felt at the gorgeous prospect before him. Barts, lords, Admirals? Pah! It must have seemed that he'd not lived till that moment! Even the Blackheath Golf Club with its quite genuine duke paled before the coming blaze.

▶ Our narrator was at his kind friend's, Lord St Vincent, when this visit was talked of, and he expressed a great desire to go over in the royal yacht to accompany the crowned heads to this country. ◀

Expressed a great desire? He must have been fairly gibbering! ▶ He joined the yacht at Deal with all speed. ◀ Heavens! at what a pace he went! ▶ Lord William Fitzroy had just left her, so he succeeded to his cabin in the lord's room. ◀ Dear God this is too much! He would have a seizure! Kings, Queens, Emperors, and living in the lord's room! Oh – Oh! What more can life offer?

▶ Louis the 18th was landed in his own dominions from England by the Royal yacht; and it was truly laughable to observe the anxiety of the active Frenchmen desirous of moving their heavy, old king into the carriage brought down on the pier at Calais to receive him. Although they literally pulled him up into the carriage by main force, and nearly dragged his coat over his head, he proved, it was most evident, in their minds a miserable contrast to their late, ever active Emperor; and the chagrin in the countenances of the French was very visible. ◀

Never mind; he was a king.

▶ Our narrator and his friends met the present king on the pier, as they were walking up with some French ladies, and although they were all known to His Majesty, and an order had previously been issued by him that no one was to go on shore but those who accompanied Royalty, yet he either did not see the narrator – as he was between two French ladies covered by their then enormous large bonnets, full of white lilies – or he kindly did not wish to observe him and he proceeded up safe into the lower town . . . ◀

Not even Napoleon at the height of his powers could have stopped Sir T. Lee then; and Henrietta Lee is half admiring and half appalled at the thought of Papa crouching feverishly between the fluttering dames, bobbing as they bobbed, till the danger was past.

But it was worth it! Oh yes, indeed. He acquired a handshake from old Prince Blucher who had arrived with some Cossack guards belonging to the Emperor of Russia. ▶ These brave men soon knew the English officers, and each time they met them drew up in a line, put their hands by their sides, and did not change a muscle till the narrator and his friends had passed. A few francs given to them at first to get some drink ensured this same attention wherever and as often as the British officers met them. ◀

Sir T. Lee says this in a tone to imply that never was money better spent; but it seems plain to Henrietta – if not to her Papa – that the Cossacks were on to a good thing. She sniggers slightly as she fancies them, stiff as a row of pokers, endlessly popping out of nowhere with the confident expectation of more francs.

At last the Emperor of Russia arrived and the whole starry gathering set sail for England where they were greeted with a rapture that was astonishing; ▶ Thousands and tens of thousands were crowding the beach in their holiday clothes ... and the Emperor of Russia said that every man appeared to be dressed like a gentleman and that he could not distinguish the poor from the rich ... ◀

But then his Imperial Majesty had not Sir T. Lee's fine eye. Our narrator could have picked a peer at five hundred paces ...

There followed now a time of delirious rapture as Sir T. Lee bounced from Crowned Head to Crowned Head like some frantic billiard ball. By some complex and astonishing manœuvre, he shook hands with the Emperor of Russia — catching him in the very act of getting out of his carriage. At last, the climax of the whole affair arrived in the exalted presence of the Prince Regent himself.

▶ The Regent walked up the street from the landing place at the Sally-port ... with the Emperor of Russia leaning on his right, and the King of Prussia on his left arm; and it must be confessed, every Englishman could not but feel proud of the elegant person of the British ruler who suffered no disadvantage from comparison with the youthful and dignified Emperor Alexander, or the King of Prussia. ◀

Then they all sailed away home. Then that awful monster Bonaparte escaped from his exile on Elba and all the fat men came quaking back again, a moving mountain of stars and sweat. But it was only for a hundred days; Waterloo extinguished the baleful genius (and with him, the Blackheath's Golf Club's solitary duke).

So the Duke of Brunswick went to Paradise, Napoleon went to St Helena, and our narrator went to Plymouth on a visit to his aunt, ▶ and on his arrival at the Royal Hotel had the pleasing adventure of arriving there only a few hours after the landing of Prince Lucien Bonaparte, from a ship going with him to America. Dr Stokoe, an old acquaintance who was attached as physician to the suite, at our narrator's urgent request . . . ◄

He met him. It was really quite uncanny. ► Every day the narrator breakfasted and dined with the Prince and Princess . . . The Prince hesitated not to enter with the greatest freedom on all points of the life and actions of his illustrious brother – the Emperor Napoleon; and what struck the narrator most forcibly was the indignation with which Lucien spoke of Prince Eugène; saying that he had betrayed his benefactor and ruined his cause – that Eugène bartered away the army of Italy at a moment when its expected assistance would have saved Napoleon; and he further added that not one of the Bonapartean family then spoke to Eugène . . . This perfectly astonished the narrator as he had ever been led to consider that Prince Eugène was a model of gratitude and fidelity to Napoleon . . . but Prince Lucien denied this *in toto* . . . The anxiety of the narrator to obtain some of the writing of Napoleon was great . . . so Prince Lucien's secretary was accordingly dispatched on board and brought on shore five or six lines of a part of Napoleon's memoirs. A small piece of the hair of Napoleon was also given with the writing to the narrator, who considers it a valuable acquisition . . . ◄

The Prince seemed to have been suspiciously free with his great brother's hair. Henrietta wonders how he came by it – and how much he had tucked away in his writing desk in his cabin, neatly labelled for dispensing to the Sir T. Lees of the world? Did he, Delilah-like, creep upon the great man while he slept and, with a pair of envious shears, snip him bald?

Perhaps it had indeed been so, and with his scattered locks had gone his superhuman strength so that the raging ogre had been subdued to the plump, memory-infested Corsican, playing with impudent children on a distant isle. An agreeable, likeable, family sort of fellow with a touch of pride, but with no more dangerous ambition than that of becoming an English country squire. He'd declared it so . . . but alas! the uneasy fat men, back in their golden jobs, would have none of it. His hair might grow again, and in England's pleasant woods and fields might arise the fearful ogre who would smash the railings, burn the fences and stamp his own unholy name on the links of the people's chains. And *then* where would the fat men go?

A pity. Henrietta sighs wistfully. Napoleon would have been a fascinating neighbour – for surely he would have settled nearby. She half sees him, all piercing-eyed, famous hand thrust in famous breast, riding up the drive to talk over old times with Sir T. Lee. Then the dream fades and all that is left is Papa, prosing on.

How odd that he should be real and the great Napoleon a dream; and odder still that he should have succeeded in the very ambition in which the world's giant had failed, and still kept his conquests intact. For here he stands, in the midst of his empire of memories, bidding them dance to his tune whenever he chooses. His domain is vast and stretches far beyond the grave. No one can exile him, for they know they would only be exiling themselves. All who enter his presence become directly a part of his grand collection, to be hung in the drawing-room or the attic, according to taste and the size of the bribe.

▶ In 1827, during the reign of George IV, the honor of Knighthood was conferred upon the narrator; and he received also the Legion of Honor from Louis 18th . . . The Emperor of Russia also sent him a superb gold vase . . . inscribed, 'This vase was presented to Sir Theophilus Lee in testimony of the high esteem and satisfaction of the Emperor of Russia'. The King of Prussia also presented him with a superb Dresden china vase, two feet high, most elaborately gilt and painted; having on one side a portrait of the king in regimentals (an excellent likeness), and on the reverse a beautiful finished drawing of Berlin. The King of Prussia has since very kindly sent another, still more splendid vase through Baron Bulow, who told the writer that the king desired to add that he well remembered him when in England. The King of Sweden also sent, through his Ambassador, a ring with his crown and initials in diamonds on blue enamel, surmounted by one hundred and sixteen other diamonds . . . ◀ (Henrietta smiles as she remembers Papa counting them several times, and getting a different answer each time.)

There would have been something from Denmark too, but for an unfortunate remark on the Royal Yacht back in 1814.

▶ A Danish nobleman, Count Molctz, asked the narrator what ship that was, meaning a frigate, the *Nymphen*, then passing under the bows of the yacht; the reply was thoughtlessly made, it was one of your ships captured at Copenhagen. The effect was in a moment most visible, he sighed deeply, and immediately went to the other side of the deck. It gave great pain to the narrator that such a reply had been incautiously given, and it was so expressed to the Count; but not anything could remove the remembrance of that event. ◄

Consequently there was not even an egg cup from Denmark; but Count Molctz is in the attic and his king is nowhere at all.

► The writer's health having now begun to fail, in consequence of the severe mental labour to which his official duties subjected him, resigned his situation . . . and his present Majesty [William IV], then Lord High Admiral, ordered him a liberal pension. ◄

But the illness passed. It was as if Death, his old respected Acquaintance, had only begged to be remembered along with the rest; and, as a further evidence of goodwill, took away a relative, one John Francis Law, ► by which several thousands of pounds came to the narrator ◄, doubtless inscribed, "In testimony of the high esteem and satisfaction of Death."

► Mr Law's death having increased the fortune of the narrator to all the extent he desired, he purchased an estate at Bedhampton in Hampshire . . . when his illustrious connection, the immortal hero, the Duke of Wellington, immediately . . . appointed him a magistrate . . . He is now in five commissions of the peace, which is always honourable . . .

His Majesty [William IV] being at this time at Brighton, the narrator drove over to pay his respects and duty; and having left his name at the Pavilion, a note was sent to the Albion Hotel to say that the king wished to see him at one o'clock. Accordingly, at the hour specified he attended at the Palace and was immediately led to the room where His Majesty was sitting . . . His Majesty then honoured him with a private interview that lasted near an hour and a half. The King spoke of the writer's father's life having been saved by His Majesty when attacking a mud fort in America . . . His Majesty kindly asked our narrator if he had ever seen the Pavilion . . . and pointed out to him the great music saloon and other apartments; after which he withdrew. On returning, he missed his way and was wandering from one room to another when he again met His Majesty . . . ◀

Anyone else might have found themselves in the kitchens; but Sir T. Lee, with the instinct of a homing pigeon, found himself back with His Majesty.

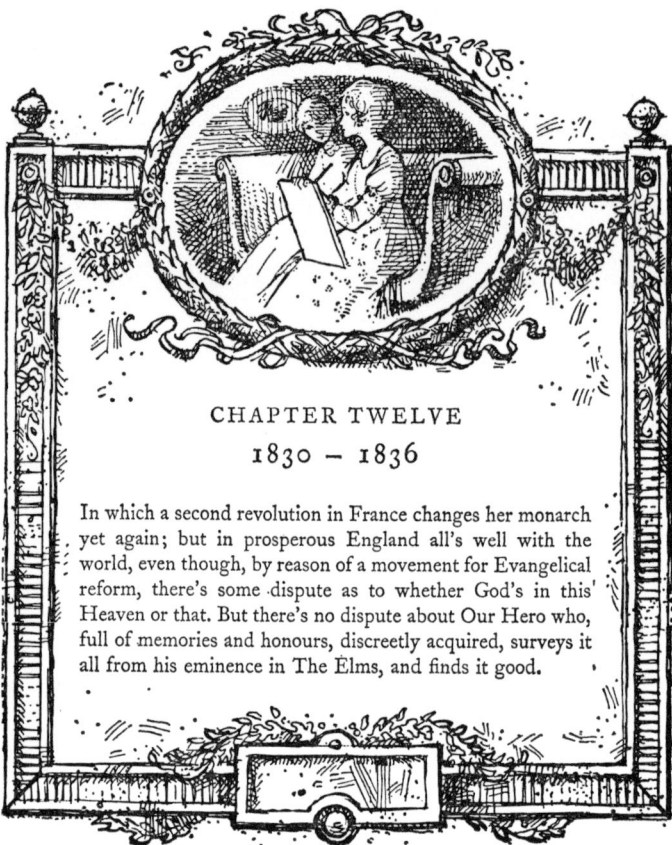

CHAPTER TWELVE
1830 — 1836

In which a second revolution in France changes her monarch
yet again; but in prosperous England all's well with the
world, even though, by reason of a movement for Evangelical
reform, there's some dispute as to whether God's in this
Heaven or that. But there's no dispute about Our Hero who,
full of memories and honours, discreetly acquired, surveys it
all from his eminence in The Elms, and finds it good.

▶THE narrator was . . . elected a Member of the
Linnaean Society and an Honorary Member of the
Philosophical Society at Devizes. He is also a Member
of the Western Yacht Club — President of the Bromp-
ton Grammar School — and President of the Brompton
Archery Club . . .◀

It's no use. Henrietta cannot get Napoleon out of
her mind. The weird notion of the Corsican genius as

an English country gentleman continues to haunt her mind. Sometimes this vision becomes so sharp that she actually sees and hears him, right in the room. "The narrator was elected First Consul . . . He is also Emperor of the French – Protector of the Confederation of the Rhine – and brother to the King of Westphalia – "

▶ The Order of the Red Eagle has since been given to the narrator and Charles Albert, King of Sardinia . . . has sent him a costly and beautiful medallion . . . ◀

"Victor of Lodi, victor of Marengo," dreams Henrietta, irresistibly, "victor of Austerlitz; came second at Waterloo . . ." Waterloo. She sees the face darken, hears the voice grow bitter as abruptly, the tide turns.

▶ A scene awaited him, and that from a source he never expected it would or could have sprung, that gave him more uneasiness than he had ever before experienced and which is the most unpleasant event of his life to detail. ◀

Napoleon at Waterloo? Bruyes at Aboukir? Villeneuve at Trafalgar, perhaps? No. Sir T. Lee at Bedhampton.

▶ So much has been said in the way of malevolent misrepresentation of his actions, and the worst feelings have been evinced by a class of men whose example in such cases should be very different . . . ◀

Not the loss of his children, not the slaughter on the Nile, not even the hanging of Patrick McCrink has moved him as deeply as this. His face darkens, his voice grows more and more bitter, and there is about him such an air of the treacherously wounded giant that were all the world his St Helena, he would still chafe at its confines. Nevertheless, he forces himself to continue, and, with dignified forbearance, tells of the fearful quarrel and mortal enmity that scorched the air of Hampshire when he persuaded the Bishop to order his clergy to give their parishioners a second service on the Sabbath day.

▶ This was the front and bearing of all the narrator's offence; and he, who through life had borne an irreproachable character, and who was, and is now, beloved and respected by some of the first noblemen and naval officers in the kingdom, was traduced by calumny for this act only, more than ever man was defamed. Statements of the most false and diabolical description were invented and disseminated . . . ◀

Tears stand in Sir T. Lee's eyes and, as he mentions the love of the first noblemen and naval officers in the kingdom, Henrietta thinks of them embracing him like the Old Guard bidding farewell to Napoleon at Fontainebleau.

▶ But he surmounted all these infamous attacks, and only desists from telling the whole statement of the cause, which brought down on him the most malignant feelings he has endured, from a desire not to appear revengeful, even in defending himself against such bitter enemies; for his conduct on this occasion most good men will feel he deserved credit, rather than enmity, from the clergy. ◀

No general could have been more magnanimous in victory . . . Suddenly, Henrietta has an idea. She leans forward, pushing Sophia urgently aside. She takes up her pencil and, with parted lips and shining eyes, begins to draw. Sophia watches, at first uneasily, but

then with growing admiration. Yes . . . yes . . . John
Lee leaves the sideboard and drifts curiously towards
his artistic sisters. He gazes over their shoulders at the
portrait. Slowly, he nods . . .

▶ The members of the Royal Western Yacht Club, ◀
continues Sir T. Lee, exhausted by his late emotion,
but nevertheless struggling courageously on, ▶ have
also lately elected Sir T. Lee Vice-President of the
Club. ◀

His voice is scarcely more than a whisper now, but
everyone thinks the Yacht Club members made a good
choice. Euphemia Lee, hungry again, has been eyeing
the sideboard, but is distracted by her elder brother's
leaving it. Inquisitively, she rises and creaks across the
floor to join him over the portrait. At first she frowns,
having some talent herself; then she, too, nods and
smiles.

▶ On the reigning Duke of Brunswick lately coming
to this country, ◀ whispers Sir T. Lee with extraordinary endurance and determination, ▶ Sir T. Lee . . .
invited him to The Elms. ◀ His voice dwindles almost
to silence. ▶ His Royal Highness, by an autograph
letter, acknowledged the attention and sent an elegant
gold snuff box as a token of His Royal Highness' regard
for Sir T. Lee. ◀

Emma and Alfred, briefly colliding, have joined the
little group about the portrait. They crane their necks,
look thoughtful, and smile . . .

▶ He now lives happy in the enjoyment of every
blessing with his dear — his beloved family at The
Elms, which sweet spot, commanding so fine a view
of the sea and Spithead, is just suited to his pleasure
and wants; and where he hopes to spend the remain-

der of his days in peace and goodwill with all the world. ◀

Henrietta lays down her pencil and Charlotte Augusta lays down her pen. The portrait and the Memoir are finished. Charlotte Augusta stands up and offers her mother her arm. Lady Lee smiles and, together with her studious daughter, joins the rest of the family. They too gaze down on Henrietta and Sophia's masterpiece. Charlotte Augusta nods directly; but Lady Lee is not quite sure. Henrietta looks to her mother enquiringly, anxiously; but still Lady Lee gives no sign. Instead, she continues to gaze at the portrait, with occasional glances at the tumbled heap of writing paper on Charlotte Augusta's table. Then her gaze shifts and she stares at her husband – who has not yet been given the artists' permission to move. Little by little his outlines seem to soften and his features gain a mysterious depth as past and present coincide and overlay each other. Again she sees the hopeful child, so alive, so tender, so eager to be liked; and then she sees him drowned in blood, so that thereafter it is a ghost that has to be nourished and fed such things as only ghosts can flourish on: reflections of glory, reflections, reflections . . . Lady Lee sighs, and fancies that she, like many another, was widowed at the Battle of the Nile, or thereabouts . . . Then she looks to Henrietta, and nods her head; yes, dear, perhaps . . .

There is a noise of something falling, then a fearful grinding as of someone treading on glass. It is Melville Lee who, impatient to join the family, has decided not to wait for the room to stop revolving. Consequently he has knocked over a side table and trodden on the empty decanter of claret. Nervously, for he is astonishingly damp with meat jelly and claret, his sisters part to let him through. He stares down until at last he manages to focus his eyes on the portrait.

He likes it; yes, he likes it very much. It's Papa to the life. He feels he ought to say something complimentary, but he cannot arrange his thoughts. Perhaps he ought to sing? Yes, that's it, a song. He draws in his breath, and before anyone can stop him, he starts, in a loud and queasy tenor, to sing the Marseillaise!

Everyone looks at him in disgust; but Melville Lee, full of French wine, goes bravely on, with his eyes fixed admiringly on the finished portrait of Sir John Theophilus Lee. Elegantly drawn, Papa gazes quizzically up; the right hand that had caused so much despair now thrust firmly out of sight in the proud, imperious breast. The attitude is unmistakable – even without the cocked hat. The Napoleon of Hampshire; the Emperor of The Elms, 1836.

Some Important Dates

1787	J. T. Lee born at Modbury, Devon
1789	Storming of Bastille by Paris mob
1790	Earl Howe devises flag signal code for ships of war
1792	J. T. Lee joins the *Cambridge* at Plymouth
1793	France at war with Great Britain, Holland, Prussia, Spain, Austria. Louis XVI executed. Pitt Prime Minister
1793–1794	Reign of Terror in France
1794	Earl Howe wins Battle of First of June
1795	Holland, Prussia and Spain withdraw from the Coalition with Britain
1795	J. T. Lee joins *Barfleur* and sails with Convoy
1796	Spain declares war on Britain
1797	Mutinies at Spithead and Nore. Admiral Jervis wins Battle of St Vincent, at which Lee serves. Lee's father appointed to the *Camel* on promotion to Captain. Lee joins him, but subsequently cruises in the *Aurora*. Admiral Duncan wins Battle of Camperdown. Lee joins the *Swiftsure*. Austria withdraws from Coalition
1798	Admiral Nelson wins Battle of Nile, at which Lee serves. Russia, Naples and Turkey join Coalition with Britain and Austria rejoins. Napoleon becomes First Consul of France
1799	Austria withdraws from Coalition. Lee leaves *Swiftsure* and returns to England to study for his Lieutenant's exam
1801	Austria makes peace with France. Russia withdraws from Coalition but later makes peace with

Britain. Admiral Nelson wins Battle of Copenhagen. Pitt resigns as Prime Minister

1802   Peace of Amiens between France and Britain

1803   Britain declares war on France. Lee passes exam for Lieutenant, but decides to take a post in the Admiralty

1804   Pitt returns as Prime Minister. Napoleon becomes Emperor of the French and plans to invade Britain

1805   Admiral Nelson wins Battle of Trafalgar. Russia, Austria and Sweden join Britain, but this Coalition fails

1806   Pitt dies – Prussia defeated by France

1807   Britain blockades northern European ports and seizes Danish fleet to counteract Continental System and French alliance with Russia. Lee marries Sophia Lawlor

1808   British hold Portugal against French

1809   Sir John Moore killed at Corunna. Wellington takes command in Portugal

1810–1814   Wellington defeats French in Spain and invades France

1812–1814   War between Britain and United States

1813   Napoleon defeated. Paris captured

1814   Treaty of Paris between France and Britain and her allies. Napoleon sent to Elba

1815   Napoleon escapes from Elba and takes up arms again, but is ultimately defeated at Waterloo and sent to St Helena. Lee attends visit of Czar of Russia and King of Prussia to England

1827   Lee knighted

1828   Lee receives a legacy after death of Francis Law and retires to the Elms at Bedhampton

Glossary

ACRE Following his victorious land campaign in Egypt, Napoleon focused his attention on Syria and launched an attack on Acre in 1799. The city was gallantly defended under the leadership of Commodore Sir Sidney Smith and the Ship's Company of the *Tigre*, and of Colonel M. Phelippeaux of the engineers, and Napoleon was eventually repulsed, after a long and desperate siege.

ANCHOR Ships have always been designed to carry their anchors in the bows and are normally anchored from this point of the ship. In an emergency, an eighteenth-century sailing warship could be anchored from the stern, but this was a difficult manœuvre to carry out and quite probably the anchor would not hold well. The cable was led along the deck and out through the stern gun ports, where the anchor was attached. The anchor was then let go and the ship allowed to ride to it. A spring or light cable could then be made fast to the cable and to the bows or midships. By heaving on the spring the ship could be swung and her guns brought to bear on a target.

Some of Nelson's captains used this tactic at the Battle of the Nile where they had a following wind and where they were obliged to anchor rapidly with shallow water to landward. Had the captains tried to anchor by the bows they would have been forced to make a long slow turn towards the wind, exposing their ships, particularly the weakly armed bows, to enemy fire which they would not have been able fully to return. Also the captains knew they did not have sufficient depth of water to allow the long sweeping turn which a sailing warship made.

BILLS DRAWN ON LISBON
Cheques which could be encashed at a bank in Lisbon.

BONNET ROUGE
The red cap worn by French citizens at the time of the Revolution as a symbol of their revolutionary fervour. It became the symbol of social justice.

CATHEADS
Heavy beams protruding from each side of the bows of a ship and fitted with sheaves like pulleys, so that they resembled fixed cranes. They were used to lift the anchor clear of the water and to suspend it clear from the ship's side before stowage.

COMMISSARY
The French equivalent of a purser, the officer who has charge of a ship's provisions and general stores.

CONVOY

A fleet of merchant ships escorted by a number of warships, all of which would be under the command of the senior naval officer, who could thus co-ordinate the defence of all ships in the most effective manner. In time of war merchant ships sailing alone were and still are very vulnerable to enemy attack.

Convoy Acts were passed 1793, 1798 and 1803 and there were standing instructions issued to escort commanders which were used earlier in the century. Except for specially armed and licensed vessels, all ships had to sail in convoy or, after 1803, forfeit their insurance. Large convoys, often made up of several small convoys sailing together, were the usual rule, to enable a strong force of escorting vessels, of which there was a shortage to be provided. Thus, the "Western Trade" vessels met together off St Helen's in the Isle of Wight, proceeded down-Channel under the guardianship of the fleet, or a heavy escort, until clear of the 100-fathom line, where the heavy escort departed if circumstances were favourable. The large convoy sailed together as long as convenient and then divided into smaller convoys for the various trades, West Indies, and so forth. It was a large convoy of this nature that thrilled John Lee when he joined his father's ship, the *Barfleur*, acting as escort whilst on passage to the Mediterranean.

COPENHAGEN

(See page 76.) Sir John Lee was referring to ships captured by Nelson after he had defeated the Danes at the Battle of Copenhagen in 1801.

COT AND COT
CLEWS

A bed made of a mattress on a wooden frame surrounded by canvas sides, ends and bottom, and suspended by clews, an arrangement of light lines hooked to the beams in the deck head (i.e. ceiling) of a cabin. Cots were normally only used by officers and measured about 6' long, 2'–3' wide and 1' deep.

TO CUT THE CABLE

To cut the anchor cable of a ship.

ENSIGN

A large flag hoisted on a staff at the stern of a ship to denote her nationality. At the time of the Napoleonic Wars the Red, White and Blue Ensigns were all used by the Royal Navy and denoted the different squadrons into which fleets were divided.

FIRE BALLS

An early form of shell; a hollow cannonball filled with explosive and ignited by a fuse, so that it would explode, as opposed to the normal solid cannonball.

GANYMEDE

The name of the cup bearer to the mythical Greek god Zeus and commonly used to mean a pot boy.

SIR THEOPHILUS LEE, K.I.H. K.R.E. F.L.S.

Deputy Lieut.^t & Magistrate for Counties of Middlesex Hants &c. &c.&c.

Portrait drawn by Henrietta and Sophia Lee.

Tower of Mirabou near Alexandria in Egypt.

Two of Lee's own drawings of the *Swiftsure*

Sectional view of a First Rate ship

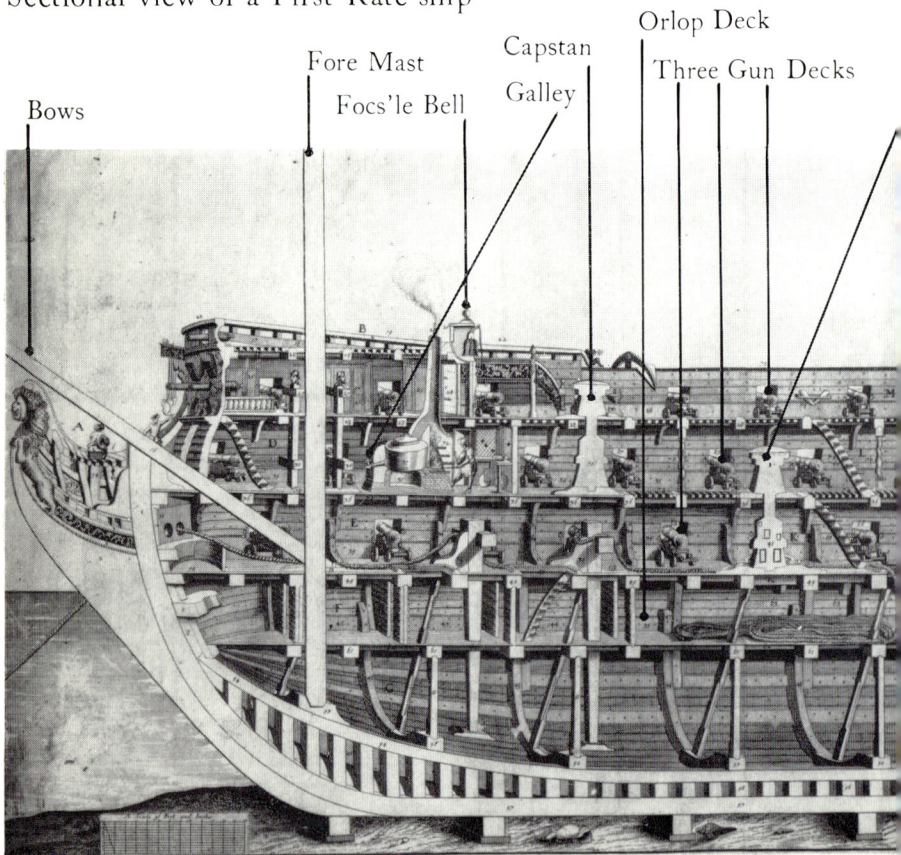

Bows

Fore Mast

Focs'le Bell

Capstan

Galley

Orlop Deck

Three Gun Decks

H.M. SHIP SWIFTSURE.

having run down from Gibraltar to attack the Spanish Gun Boats near Algeziras and protect a Convoy, is becalmed and suffered severely.

Main Mast

Capstan   Hold   Quarter Deck

Mizzen Mast
Gun Room Area
Ward Room

Admiral's Cabin
Captain's Cabin
Stern
Poop

L'Orient exploding at The Battle of the Nile. The *Swiftsure* is on the right. Oil painting by G. Arnald.

GLASS — A telescope.

JACK — Nickname commonly given to a British sailor.

LANTHORN — A lantern, lit by oil or candle light.

LARBOARD — The port side of a ship; the left when the viewer stands on deck facing the bows.

LEE SIDE — The side of a ship opposite to that on which the wind is blowing.

LEMON JUICE — Regular consumption of lemon juice was the most effective preventive against scurvy. Scurvy was the dreadful disease that attacked seamen and decimated crews who lacked proper diet in the days when it was not possible to preserve fresh supplies easily. Selling supplies of lemon juice was profitable and always open to abuse by dishonest merchants and officials.

LETTERS OF MARQUE — Official documents issued by the Lords of the Admiralty which licensed captains of armed merchant ships to act as though their ships were warships independent of the fleet. Their purpose was to harry and capture enemy shipping. They could gain prize-money thereby. Armed private merchant ships or privateers often used the possession of official letters of marque to prey upon enemy shipping during time of war, sometimes quite indiscriminately. In some cases the line between privateering and piracy became practically indistinguishable.

MARSEILLAISE

(La Marseillaise.) The French national anthem originally composed in 1792 by Claude de Lisle to serve as a marching song for the revolutionary troops.

NAPLES

When John Lee was alive Naples was the capital of the independent Neapolitan Kingdom, not simply an important city in Italy.

THE NILE, BATTLE OF

After a search which lasted some two months (June and July 1798), and which involved the whole Mediterranean area, Nelson found the French naval squadron, which had escorted the transports for Napoleon's army of Egypt, anchored in Aboukir Bay, to the west of the Nile Delta. Although it was late in the day, when one did not normally fight on wooden ships because of the risk of fire at night, Nelson's captains went straight into the attack. His squadron of thirteen ships of the line, one fifty-gun ship and one brig faced the more heavily armed French squadron of thirteen ships of the line and four frigates. The fighting began at 6 p.m. on August 1st, and lasted all night and into the next morning. The British had the advantage of mobility and surprise because of the rapidity of their attack; because in the early stages they concentrated all their force on the leading French ships and because they attacked not only from the seaward side of the French line but also from the landward side, catching the French in a cross fire.

Lee's ship, the *Swiftsure*, did not start firing until 8 p.m. when she was placed between two French ships. Later she attacked the giant French flagship *L'Orient*, which had previously been engaged by the *Bellerophon*. The *Swiftsure* came closer to the *L'Orient* in an attempt to avoid the cascade of burning debris which Captain Hallowell realized would gush out of the *L'Orient* when she exploded.

The peril of Commodore Casabianca and his ten-year-old son aboard the burning *L'Orient* just before she exploded gave rise to the poem:

"The boy stood on the burning deck,
Whence all but he had fled;
The flame that lit the battle's wreck
Shone round him o'er the dead."

By the morning all the French ships except two had been destroyed, captured or put out of action. The remaining two escaped, to be captured later.

PACKET

A vessel sailing on a pre-arranged route and carrying mails. The packet ships were usually quite small, but they could carry passengers. A naval officer's family could travel in this way to keep him company when he was serving overseas.

PRIZE MONEY

Captured enemy ships, both merchant and naval, were called prizes. By the system of prize money, a captured enemy ship and her cargo were sold and the money so gained was shared out in proportions amongst the crew of the victorious ship. By the Act of 1793, a Captain received a $\frac{3}{8}$ share, Lieutenants and Midshipmen equal shares in a $\frac{1}{8}$ share.

In 1971 the value of a pound is about nine times as great as it was in Lee's time. The buying power of the £600 prize money gained by the seamen of the *Aurora* would be the equivalent of about £5,400 today.

RAKING

Firing into an enemy ship from such a position that the broadside of the raking ship is aimed down the length of her opponent, taking advantage of the weak bulkheads at the bow or stem of a wooden warship and of the fact that the defending ship cannot use her broadside in reply.

ROCHETTS

The Earl of St Vincent's home in Essex.

ROUNDJACKET

To make their tailcoats more practical garments for wear at sea, officers often cut off the tails. The resultant jacket or a similar purpose-designed garment was called a roundjacket and resembled the style of men's jackets today.

ST VINCENT, BATTLE OF

The Battle of St Vincent was fought between the Spanish fleet of twenty-six ships of the line and nine frigates and the British fleet of fifteen ships of the line and six frigates under the command of Sir John Jervis, on February 14th, 1797, off Cape St Vincent on the SW tip of the Coast of Portugal. During the early stages of the battle, the British fleet in one line cut through the Spanish formation. For a while there was a risk that the two divisions of the Spanish fleet might rejoin and sail away before the British line had time to turn and launch a full attack. At this point, Commodore Horatio Nelson left the line without orders and placed his ship *Captain* across the line of advance of the second Spanish division. This tactic, supported by Sir John Jervis who ordered Captain Collingwood in the *Excellent* to assist Nelson, brought on the main action, during which four Spanish ships were captured. By 4.30 p.m. the fighting had almost ended and both sides lay to during the night to repair damage. After some manœuvring on the following day the Spanish sailed away to take refuge in Cadiz, where after a respite in Lagos Bay the British blockaded them. John Lee's ship the *Barfleur* was tenth ship in the attacking line.

Many of the terms used by John Lee to describe the different points of sailing are difficult to understand although they are similar to those used by yachtsmen today.

Haul up: to pull at a single rope without the help of mechanical aids, blocks or the like. In the case of a ship it can mean to trim the sails and yards so as to sail closer to the wind. "To haul her wind" has the same meaning in the case of a ship.

Bear up: to put the helm of a sailing ship up, so that she turns away from the wind.

Shorten sail: to reduce the number of sails set.

Heave to: to adjust the sails of a ship so that they counteract each other and thereby stop the ship moving. The ship is then said to be *lying to the wind*. In a gale, "to heave to" normally means to carry enough sail to steady the ship.

Under easy sail: to reduce the amount of sail so that the ship sails easily, but not at her fastest. In the *Aurora* Captain Digby lowered the fore and mizen top gallant masts, which had the effect of disguising the appearance of the ship, as well as making her sail easily.

TO SNAP A PIECE — In this context (page 65) to fire a flint-lock musket; "snap" expressing the sound of the flint hitting the steel.

SPRINGS — Light hawsers leading from the side of a ship attached to a fixed object on shore or to the heavy anchor cable so that a ship could be slewed and the direction of (aim of) her broadside of guns altered.

STARBOARD — The right side of ship when the viewer stands on deck facing the bows.

SWABS — Long mops made of old rope used for cleaning the decks. Also a term of abuse for lower deck hands.

VAN — The leading or front ships of a fleet or squadron.

VICTUALS — Provisions for a ship.

WEATHER SIDE — The side of a ship on which the wind blows.

Acknowledgments

The publishers wish to acknowledge their gratitude to the Trustees and Director of the National Maritime Museum, London, for so generously making the original memoir of Sir J. T. Lee available to Leon Garfield and for permitting David Proctor, who is Education Officer to the Museum, to assist him as consultant. The illustrations have been drawn from the collections at the Museum and the publishers are grateful for this additional help. Readers who would like to see more material illustrating the time and ships in which Lee lived are invited to pay a visit to the Museum, where excellent examples are on display in the galleries.